CHARLES DICKENS

Bleak House

GRAHAM STOREY

Fellow of Trinity Hall and Reader in English, University of Cambridge

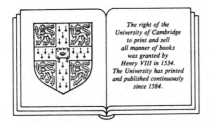

The right of the
University of Cambridge
to print and sell
all manner of books
was granted by
Henry VIII in 1534.
The University has printed
and published continuously
since 1584.

CAMBRIDGE UNIVERSITY PRESS

Cambridge
London   New York   New Rochelle
Melbourne   Sydney

Published by the Press Syndicate of the University of Cambridge
The Pitt Building, Trumpington Street, Cambridge CB2 1RP
32 East 57th Street, New York, NY 10022, USA
10 Stamford Road, Oakleigh, Melbourne 3166, Australia

First published 1987

Printed in Great Britain at
the University Press, Cambridge

British Library cataloguing in publication data

Storey, Graham
Charles Dickens: Bleak House – (Landmarks of
world literature)
1. Dickens, Charles, *1812–1870*. Bleak House
I. Title   II. Dickens, Charles, *1812–1870*
Bleak House   III. Series
823′.8   PR4556

Library of Congress cataloguing in publication data

Storey, Graham, 1920–
Charles Dickens – Bleak House
(Landmarks of world literature)
Bibliography.
1. Dickens, Charles, 1812–1870. Bleak House.
I. Title. II. Series
PR4556.S86   1987   832′.8   86–271

ISBN 0 521 32817 9 hard covers
ISBN 0 521 31691 X paperback

VN

Contents

Chronology   *page* vi

1 *Bleak House*: the background   1
     Historical context   1
     Intellectual context   10

2 *Bleak House*: the novel   16
     Structure: the double narrative   16
     Language   32
     Social groups   48
     Irony   68
     Set-scenes   76

3 Critical reception   86

4 Context in European literature   94

Guide to further reading   108

Chronology

	Dickens's life and works	Related literary and historical events
1811		W. M. Thackeray born.
1812	Born at 387 Mile End Terrace, Portsea, Hampshire (7 February).	
1814		Walter Scott's first novel, *Waverley*.
1815		Napoleon defeated at Waterloo.
1819		John Ruskin and George Eliot (Mary Ann Evans) born. The 'Peterloo Massacre' (16 August), in which the militia charged a Manchester reform meeting, killing eleven and injuring about 600. George IV succeeds to the throne.
1820	At William Giles's 'Classical, Mathematical and Commercial School', Chatham, Kent.	
1824	Works for about four months in Warren's Blacking Factory, Hungerford Stairs, London, during his father's imprisonment for debt in the Marshalsea.	
1824–5	At Wellington House Academy, Hampstead Road, London	
1827	Solicitor's clerk in Messrs Ellis & Blackmore, Gray's Inn.	

1828	Moves to Messrs Charles Molloy, Lincoln's Inn.
1829	Reporter in Doctors' Commons.	Honoré de Balzac's *La Comédie Humaine* begins. Robert Peel establishes the Metropolitan Police. William IV succeeds to the throne.
1830–3	Unsuccessful love affair with Maria Beadnell.	
1832	Reporter on the *True Sun* newspaper (March–July). Reporter on his uncle J. H. Barrow's paper, *Mirror of Parliament*.	Jeremy Bentham dies. Passing of the Reform Bill. Sir Walter Scott dies.
1833	First sketch, 'A Dinner at Poplar Walk', published in the *Monthly Magazine* (December).	Thomas Carlyle's *Sartor Resartus*. First Factory Act makes it illegal for children under nine to work in factories and for children between nine and thirteen to work more than a nine-hour day.
1834	Staff reporter on *Morning Chronicle*; contributes several 'street sketches' to it.	S. T. Coleridge dies. The 'Tolpuddle Martyrs', six Dorsetshire labourers, transported to Australia for taking an illegal oath to a trade union; pardoned after two years.
1835	Contributes 'Sketches of London' to *Evening Chronicle*.	Abolition of slavery in the British Empire.
1836	*Sketches by Boz*. Marries Catherine Hogarth (2 April). *The Strange Gentleman* and *The Village Coquettes* produced at St James's Theatre, London. *Sunday under Three Heads*.	
1836–7	*The Pickwick Papers*.	
1837–9	Edits *Bentley's Miscellany* (magazine).	

	Dickens's life and works	Related literary and historical events
1837	*Oliver Twist* (published in *Bentley's Miscellany*). Mary Hogarth, Catherine's sister, aged seventeen, dies suddenly in the Dickens's home in Doughty Street, London (7 May). *Is She His Wife?* produced at St James's Theatre.	Victoria, aged seventeen, succeeds to the throne. Carlyle's *The French Revolution*.
1838	Edits *Memoirs of Joseph Grimaldi*, the clown.	Thackeray's *The Yellowplush Correspondence* (published in *Fraser's Magazine*). *The People's Charter* published.
1838–9	*Nicholas Nickleby.*	
1839	Moves to Devonshire Terrace, London.	First Chartist riots, on Parliament's rejection of Chartist Petition.
1840		Queen Victoria marries Prince Albert of Saxe-Coburg-Gotha. Carlyle's *Chartism.*
1840–1	*Master Humphrey's Clock*, containing *The Old Curiosity Shop* and *Barnaby Rudge.*	
1841	Edits *The Pic Nic Papers.*	Carlyle's *On Heroes and Hero Worship.* *Punch* founded; edited by Mark Lemon. Further Chartist riots.
1842	First visit to America, with Catherine (January–June).	Lord Shaftesbury's Mines and Collieries Bill, prohibiting the employment of women, and boys under thirteen, in mines and collieries.
1842–3	*Martin Chuzzlewit.*	
1843	*A Christmas Carol.*	Carlyle's *Past and Present.*

Year		
1844	In Italy. *The Chimes*.	Benjamin Disraeli's *Coningsby*. 'Ragged School' Union founded.
1845	Directs amateur production of Jonson's *Every Man in his Humour*. *The Cricket on the Hearth*.	Disraeli's *Sybil, or the Two Nations*. Engels's *The Condition of the Working Classes in England*.
1846	Launches the *Daily News*; his friend John Forster takes over as editor after two and a half weeks. In Switzerland and Paris. *The Battle of Life*.	Thackeray's *The Book of Snobs*. Lord John Russell Prime Minister, after repeal of Corn Laws.
1846–7	*Dombey and Son*.	
1847–8	Directs further amateur theatricals.	Thackeray's *Vanity Fair*.
1848	*The Haunted Man*.	Revolutions throughout Europe. Marx and Engels's *Communist Manifesto*. Chartist National Convention in London; soon disperses (10 April).
1848–50		Thackeray's *Pendennis*.
1849		Elizabeth Gaskell's *Mary Barton*. Charles Kingsley's *Alton Locke*.
1849–50	*David Copperfield*.	
1850	Founds and 'conducts' *Household Words*, a weekly journal.	Establishment in England of the Roman Catholic Hierarchy (September); Wiseman created Archbishop of Westminster and Cardinal.

	Dickens's life and works	Related literary and historical events
1851	His father dies (31 March). Produces Bulwer Lytton's comedy, *Not so Bad as we Seem*, to raise funds for the Guild of Literature and Art, founded by Lytton and himself. Writes to Miss Coutts: 'I begin to be pondering afar off, a new book' (17 August). Writes to Henry Austin of his 'new book waiting to be born' (7 September). Moves to Tavistock House, London (November). Begins to write *Bleak House* (late November).	Lord John Russell's government defeated (February); after Lord Derby fails to form a Ministry, Russell returns to office (March). The Great Exhibition, promoted by Prince Albert and housed in Joseph Paxton's Crystal Palace, in Hyde Park, opened by the Queen (1 May). Chancery Reform Bill passed (July). Lord Shaftesbury's Lodging Houses Bill passed (August).
1852–3	*Bleak House* (19/20 monthly parts, March 1852–September 1853), illustrated by H. K. Browne ('Phiz').	
1852	Acknowledges receipt of William Challinor's pamphlet, *The Court of Chancery; Its Inherent Defects as Exhibited in Its System of Written Procedures, 1849* (March). Takes *Not so Bad as we Seem* on a provincial tour, to help the Guild of Literature and Art. *A Child's History of England* (first published in *Household Words*).	General election (July). Lord Derby Conservative Prime Minister for five months; Whig coalition, under Lord Aberdeen, takes over in December. Thackeray's *History of Henry Esmond*. The Duke of Wellington dies.
1853	In Boulogne and Italy. Gives first public readings from the Christmas Books, to help the Birmingham and Midland Institute.	Elizabeth Gaskell's *Cranford* (first published in *Household Words*). Thackeray's *The Newcomes*.

1854	*Hard Times* (first published weekly in *Household Words*).	Charles Kingsley's *Westward Ho!*
1854–6		The Crimean War.
1855	Supports the Administrative Reform Association in its criticism of the conduct of the Crimean War.	
1855–7	*Little Dorrit.*	
1856	Buys Gad's Hill Place, near Rochester, Kent.	
1857	Produces and acts in Wilkie Collins's *The Frozen Deep*, first at Tavistock House; then in Manchester, where Ellen Ternan and her sister act in it.	Thackeray's *The Virginians.* The Indian Mutiny.
1858	Separates from Catherine (May). Gives first series of public readings from his works for profit.	
1859	Founds a new weekly journal, *All the Year Round*. *A Tale of Two Cities* (first published weekly in *All the Year Round*).	Leigh Hunt dies. Charles Darwin's *On the Origin of Species.* J. S. Mill's *On Liberty.*
1860	Moves to Gad's Hill Place.	Wilkie Collins's *The Woman in White.*
1860–1	*Great Expectations* (first published weekly in *All the Year Round*).	
1861		Prince Albert dies.
1861–2	Further public readings.	The American Civil War.
1861–5		J. S. Mill's *Utilitarianism.*
1862		Victor Hugo's *Les Misérables.* Ivan Turgenev's *Fathers and Sons.* John Ruskin's *Unto This Last.*

	Dickens's life and works	*Related literary and historical events*
1863	Further public readings.	Abolition of slavery in America. Thackeray dies. W. S. Landor dies.
1864	His mother dies (September).	Elizabeth Gaskell dies.
1864–5	*Our Mutual Friend.*	Sir Joseph Paxton dies.
1865	In the Staplehurst, Kent, railway accident (June).	Assassination of President Lincoln. Feodor Dostoevsky's *Crime and Punishment.*
1866		
1866–7	Further public readings.	Karl Marx's *Das Kapital*, vol. I.
1867		Second Reform Bill passed. Further Factory Acts.
1867–8	Second visit to America, to give public readings (November 1867–April 1868).	
1868	Further public readings.	Wilkie Collins's *The Moonstone.* Dostoevsky's *The Idiot.*
1868–70	Further public readings.	
1869		Imprisonment for debt abolished.
1870	The first six parts of *The Mystery of Edwin Drood* (April–September). Dies at Gad's Hill (9 June). Buried in Westminster Abbey.	W. E. Forster's Elementary Education Act, setting up a system of state education. Civil Service reformed.

Further history of *'Bleak House'*

1853 Published in one volume.
1857 Translated into French.
1858 Published in the Cheap Edition of Dickens's Works.
1860 Translated into German.
1874 Earliest recorded adaptation for the stage, *Jo*, by J. P. Barnett; first performed in California; performed in London, 1876; followed, before the end of the century, by at least six other adaptations.

Chapter 1

Bleak House: the background

Historical context

As John Butt and Kathleen Tillotson showed many years ago, in *Dickens at Work* (1957), *Bleak House* is a remarkably topical novel. No less than five of the major targets of its anger, as they show in detail, were public issues in 1851, the year in which Dickens began to write it: the abuses of the court of Chancery; the establishment the year before of the Roman Catholic hierarchy in England; political misgovernment (for a period, no government at all); the London slums; and what Dickens calls 'Telescopic philanthropy', the ignoring of crying social needs at home for the spurious excitement of sending out missions abroad.

It is true that neither the appalling conditions of the London poor nor the abuses of Chancery were new subjects for Dickens. Jacob's Island in *Oliver Twist* is the first of his London slums; Want and Ignorance are the children who, in a vision, convert Scrooge in *A Christmas Carol*, his first Christmas book; a long passage in *Dombey and Son* cries out against the horrifying effects of bad sanitation. The most serious and pathetic point (as Dickens described it in a letter of December 1852) that he had tried to make in *Pickwick* was the lingering death of a Chancery prisoner. What makes *Bleak House* a landmark, the first of Dickens's 'dark period' novels, is that, for the first time, he has created a whole world out of such and similar evils. It is the whole of contemporary society that he anatomizes. Of his peculiar gift for seeing connexions between things not glimpsed by most people he was fully aware: 'I think', he wrote to his friend Lord Lytton in 1865, with a touch of irony, 'it is my infirmity to fancy or perceive relations in things which are not apparent generally'.

These five major issues, then, constitute the true historical background to *Bleak House*. Together they form what Thomas Carlyle, the most powerful intellectual influence on Dickens, had called, in *Chartism* (1840), the 'Condition-of-England question'; and, more vehemently in *Past and Present* (1843), where he analyses the consequences of failing to solve it, 'universal social gangrene'. To understand the novel's impact on its first readers we must grasp the immediacy of each of these issues and the precision – and intensity – with which Dickens deals with them. In a novel pervaded by irony, the title *Bleak House* itself is surely a parody of the major English event of 1851, the Great Exhibition: the grim reality beneath the materialistic complacency, the boasted 'commerce of all nations'.

The opening chapter, 'In Chancery', brilliantly suggests the novel's universal blight; its centre, the case of Jarndyce and Jarndyce, being heard, as it has been for many years, by the Lord Chancellor in the High Court of Chancery, was highly topical too. Chancery abuse had been a target for reformers for several decades; but in 1851 it had become a major national issue. 'Trickery, evasion, procrastination, spoliation, botheration . . . false pretences of all sorts . . . Shirking and sharking, in all their many varieties', as John Jarndyce puts it, are the fruits of Jarndyce and Jarndyce; almost all had been anticipated in leading anti-Chancery articles in *The Times* during 1851.

Jarndyce and Jarndyce was itself based on a notorious Chancery case, begun in 1834 and still proceeding; a similar case in Staffordshire was the model for what drove Gridley all but mad. National demands procured some reform in an Act of August 1851; for Dickens only the burning away of the Court 'in a great funeral pyre' could accomplish what he wanted and in his way achieved in 'Chancellor' Krook's spontaneous combustion.

But the language of the final paragraph describing Krook's death (ch. 32: 'The Appointed Time') goes far beyond legal reform:

[Krook] has died the death of all Lord Chancellors in all Courts, and of all authorities in all places under all names soever, where false pretences are made, and where injustice is done.

In *Past and Present*, Carlyle had painted the treatment and despair of a disappointed Chancery client as an example of general administrative futility. Dickens has gone further in both directions: he has made the most of the topical appeal of Chancery abuse to his readers; he has also made of it a symbol of universal corruption.

Even more widely discussed than Chancery abuse in 1851 was the religious crisis caused by the establishment of the Roman Catholic hierarchy in England the year before – freely referred to as 'Papal Aggression'. For Dickens, who hated the Roman Catholic Church, the Oxford Movement, the party within the Anglican Church that aimed to restore it to its primitive 'Catholic' roots, and in particular E. B. Pusey, its new Oxford leader (the 'Pusey and Newman Corporation', as Carlyle called it in a letter), were directly responsible; and they were deeply distasteful to him. In *Bleak House* he derides them. Mrs Pardiggle is not only distinguished for her 'rapacious benevolence', but is clearly a Puseyite as well: her five sons are named after saints and heroes of the primitive Church; they are taken to Matins '(very prettily done)' at 6.30 a.m. all the year round; and the little book she gives to the brickmakers is no doubt a Puseyite Tract ('It's a book fit for a babby, and I'm not a babby', says one of them). The ladies who want Jarndyce's money to house 'the Sisterhood of Medieval Marys' are clearly Puseyites too. But the most dangerous ones – equally derided – are the fashionable guests at Chesney Wold who have set up a Dandyism in Religion:

Who, in mere lackadaisical want of an emotion, have agreed upon a little dandy talk about the Vulgar wanting faith in things in general . . . Who would make the Vulgar very picturesque and faithful, by putting back the hands upon the Clock of Time, and cancelling a few hundred years of history.   (ch. 12)

For Carlyle, 'Dandy' was a favourite word of opprobrium, the opposite of the man in true earnest. *Sartor Resartus* ('the tailor re-patched'), 1833–4, his scathing discourse on the philosophy of clothes, has 'Dandyising Christians' and the 'Dandiacal Body'. Dickens is clearly following Carlyle. Here he links the Puseyite 'dandies' with another set of elegant Chesney Wold guests, 'of another fashion', 'who have agreed to put a smooth glaze on the world, and to keep down all its realities'. There is a perhaps closer link here with the dilettante aestheticism of two of the characters, Skimpole and Turveydrop. Again, the topical has its immediate point, but its implications go much further: the 'dandy' aspects of Puseyism – the High Church ritual that Dickens disliked as much as Carlyle – only too readily become the unreality that is part of the general corruption of *Bleak House*: the beginnings of that 'leprosy of unreality' that he attributes to the French *ancien régime* in *A Tale of Two Cities*.

There is yet another 'Dandyism' among the guests at Chesney Wold: the conviction of 'the brilliant and distinguished circle' that, in the choice of a Party to govern the country, 'nobody is in question but Boodle and his retinue and Buffy and *his* retinue. These are the great actors for whom the stage is reserved' (ch. 12). 'A People' there may be – but they are only stage extras; it is Boodle and Buffy who are 'the born first-actors, managers and leaders, and no others can appear upon the scene for ever and ever'. This belief of a few aristocratic families in their sacred right to govern the country – and to exclude all others, however able – was highly topical too. In February 1851, after Lord John Russell's administration was defeated, there was literally a two weeks' hiatus in government; and one reason was the Party leaders' belief that no one else could be brought in for the task. Dickens's sarcasm echoes similar attacks in *The Times*; and he begins ch. 40 ('National and Domestic') even more pointedly:

England has been in a dreadful state for some weeks. Lord Coodle would go out, Sir Thomas Doodle wouldn't come in, and there being nobody in Great Britain (to speak of) except Coodle and Doodle, there has been no Government.

The first readers of *Bleak House* would certainly have responded to the topicality of this; just as they would have done to Volumnia Dedlock's unfortunate mistake in asking Sir Leicester what the Party's 'enormous expense' in winning had been for. Bribery was still an integral part of every election.

Topicality, then, gives an extra edge to the satire of both ch. 1 ('In Chancery') and ch. 12, the description of the houseparty at Chesney Wold. But Dickens's contempt for Parliament and party politics went back far beyond 1851: it was wholly consistent from the Eatanswill election in *Pickwick Papers* to *Our Mutual Friend*. It was inevitable that the corrupt Merdle of *Little Dorrit* should be a member of Parliament, as would be the *nouveau riche* Veneering of *Our Mutual Friend*. In *Hard Times*, the novel that followed *Bleak House*, Thomas Gradgrind, the implacable enemy of imagination, is of course an M.P., and members of Parliament in general are 'the National Dustmen'. Scorn for both Parliament and Government is the refrain of many letters, particularly to Forster, in the 1850s and 1860s.

The filth, hideous overcrowding and lack of sanitation of the slums are a major part of the bleakness of *Bleak House*. Tom-all-Alone's (described in all its foulness in both chs. 16 and 46) is the most horrible: it appears, in fact, in all of the titles for the novel considered by Dickens before settling on *Bleak House*. The brickmakers' hovels near St Alban's, with their wretched and mostly drunken inhabitants, are nearly as bad. And they are reinforced by another source of evil, the rat-infested paupers' graveyard, where Captain Hawdon and Jo are both buried and Lady Dedlock dies. This was founded on fact too. It was the notorious graveyard of St Martin's-in-the-Fields, which Dickens had known as a boy. Dickens brings all these disease-bearing pollutions, and others, together – appropriately – on the night of Krook's death:

It is a fine steaming night to turn the slaughterhouses, the unwholesome trades, the sewage, bad water, and burial-grounds to account, and give the Registrar of Deaths some extra business.   (ch. 32)

Overcrowding, bad drainage, contaminated water – and the diseases they engender – were, again, highly topical issues in 1851; made worse, in many people's eyes, by the proximity and prosperity of the Great Exhibition. Dickens had attacked them as early as his terrible picture of Jacob's Island in *Oliver Twist*. He attacked them again, with the crimes they led to, in a long passage in *Dombey and Son* (ch. 17). From 1849 onwards, sanitary reform was a major subject of his public speeches and journalism: 'the most momentous of all earthly questions', he called it in his address 'To Working Men', published in *Household Words* on 7 October 1854. Cholera epidemics made it more urgent; his brother-in-law Henry Austin's work as Secretary of the General Board of Health, and the copies of the reports Austin sent him, helped to make him highly informed on the appalling problems involved. *Bleak House* not only gives hideous examples of slums and pauper graveyards; it shows how they contaminate high and low alike; that disease is no respecter of class.

Dickens gave the same grim warning in a speech at the Metropolitan Sanitary Association dinner in May 1851. In *Bleak House*, Jo's infection of Esther with smallpox shows it dramatically come true. We are not allowed to forget the cholera, either: Guster, the Snagsbys' epileptic servant, is a survivor of the 1849 Tooting 'baby-farm' scandal, in which 180 pauper children died from cholera and neglect (Dickens devoted four articles in the *Examiner* to exposing it). In a new Preface to *Oliver Twist*, of 1850, Dickens had written of the necessity to improve slum conditions:

I have always been convinced that this reform must precede all other Social Reforms; that it must prepare the way for Education, even for Religion; and that, without it, those classes of the people which increase the fastest must become so desperate, and be made so miserable, as to bear within themselves the certain seeds of ruin to the whole community.

The bearing of those seeds, principally by Jo, is brilliantly and horribly shown in *Bleak House*.

The last of the novel's major topical issues was what Dickens sarcastically calls 'Telescopic philanthropy', misguided benevolence abroad, which ignored the acute social problems at home. It is yet another form of blindness, seen at its most extreme and absurd in the novel's two famous 'philanthropists', Mrs Jellyby and Mrs Pardiggle. Mrs Jellyby's eyes 'had a curious habit of seeming to look a long way off. As if . . . they could see nothing nearer than Africa!' Mrs Pardiggle lavishes her family's contributions on her Tockahoopo Indians; but is utterly blind to the realities of the brickmakers' wretched lives. Jo, the destitute crossing-sweeper, sitting on the doorstep of the Society for the Propagation of the Gospel in Foreign Parts, munching 'his dirty bit of bread', makes the point even more emphatically; as does the appalling picture of his ignorance, when questioned by the Coroner at the inquest on Nemo (ch. 11). We know that this was modelled on fact, on the case of a boy named George Ruby, about fourteen years old, called, on 8 January 1850, at the Guildhall, to give evidence in a case of assault. Jo's answers to the Coroner are remarkably similar to the boy's, given in a report in Dickens's own *Household Narrative*.

Mrs Jellyby may have had her prototype in Mrs Caroline Chisholm, whose Family Colonization Loan Society for helping emigrants to Australia Dickens in fact supported, yet whose housekeeping and dirty-faced children, he wrote to Miss Coutts, haunted his dreams. But, much more than that, she is a representative of Exeter Hall, the centre of evangelical missionary activity in London, for which Dickens, like Carlyle, had a profound contempt. Her African project, to educate the natives of Borrioboola-Gha, 'on the left bank of the Niger', echoes almost exactly a disastrous expedition to the River Niger in 1841, to abolish the slave trade and to improve agriculture. Dickens had reviewed the published account of it in the *Examiner* of 19 August 1848, and had duly made the point about Exeter Hall, which had, of course, been 'hot in its behalf':

It might be laid down as a very good general rule of social and political guidance, that whatever Exeter Hall champions, is the thing by no means to be done.

The Niger expedition was a fiasco: those who survived fever were murdered by 'King Boy'; 'King Obi' returned to selling slaves. Mrs Jellyby's project was a similar disaster, 'the King of Borrioboola wanting to sell everybody – who survived the climate – for Rum'.

The moral was clear: charity, desperately needed, must begin at home. Carlyle, who had dismissed Exeter Hall for its 'rose-pink sentimentalism' in 1849, made the same point – but more vehemently – in his pamphlet 'The Nigger Question' the same year: 'Lord John Russell is able to comfort us with one fact . . . That the Negroes are all very happy and doing well; whereas at home . . . the British Whites are rather badly off; several millions of them hanging on the verge of continual famine.'

John Butt and Kathleen Tillotson point to yet another topicality in the novel's scorn for 'managing' women. In the summer of 1851 the fame of the American Mrs Bloomer, who had adopted male clothing, reached England; mockery of her and her masculine pretensions filled *Punch*. Just before beginning *Bleak House*, Dickens published a highly satirical article, 'Sucking Pigs', in *Household Words* (8 November 1851); in it he makes clear the connexion between the 'Bloomers' and the excited women's committee of *Bleak House*, ch. 8, who constantly pester the benevolent John Jarndyce for money – and his distaste for both:

even if Mrs Bellows chooses to become, of her own free will and liking, a Bloomer, that won't do. She must agitate, agitate, agitate. She must take to the little table and water-bottle. She must go in to be a public character. She must work away at a Mission. It is not enough to do right for right's sake.

The women Missioners of *Bleak House* – 'The women of England, the Daughters of Britain', and the rest – include an early archetypal feminist, Miss Wisk: *her* mission, which she preaches to Caddy's wedding breakfast party in ch. 30, was 'the emancipation of Woman from the thraldom of her Tyrant, Man'. If Dickens so patently approves of the quiet femininity of Esther, the opposite qualities that he gives to the women Missioners at least provide one good reason.

Intellectual context

Dickens was a novelist of genius, with a formidably keen intelligence and a deep understanding of his Age; he was not, as many critics have rightly stressed, an intellectual. Just as he hated most institutionalized social and political systems – as *Bleak House* and *Little Dorrit*, written three years later, emphatically show – so he had little affection for abstract systems of thought. With all his radicalism, he never, for instance, in letters or speeches, mentions Marx and Engels's *Communist Manifesto*, published in 1848. It is in fact much easier to find a coherent pattern in what he disliked than in his positive sympathies, clear though these are on every page of his writing. If such a pattern does not add up to an abstractly formulated 'philosophy', it nevertheless makes his allegiances, as well as his antipathies, abundantly clear.

The most perceptive analyst of early Victorian England, John Stewart Mill, saw two antagonistic modes of thought and feeling dividing thinking men's minds: romantic idealism, inspired by S. T. Coleridge, and philosophical radicalism, inspired by Jeremy Bentham, the ablest and best-known champion of Utilitarianism, the belief in utility as the touchstone of morality. Coleridge and Bentham were, he claimed, the 'great seminal minds of the century': 'every Englishman in the nineteenth century is by implication either a Benthamite or a Coleridgean', he wrote in *On Bentham and Coleridge*.

There have been many attempts in the past to enlist Dickens as a follower of Bentham; and many of the abuses he attacked in *Bleak House* – legal muddle and delay, corruption in government – had been Bentham's targets before. But a shared demand for reform does not make Dickens a Benthamite. He may well have been influenced by Bentham's critical radicalism, and he certainly regarded himself as a radical; but, insofar as he understood Bentham's philosophical theories, he was temperamentally strongly averse to them. Coleridge he never mentions by name, but, by implication, Dickens was emphatically a Coleridgean. He owned both Coleridge's and Wordsworth's *Poems*, besides Wordsworth's *The Prelude*; and he referred to Wordsworth's 'genius' in a diary-note in 1838, when he met his younger son. He also greatly admired the Romantic essayists, especially Lamb and Leigh Hunt (a personal friend) – despite his immortalizing Hunt as Harold Skimpole. His insistence on 'Fancy' (he could equally have called it 'Imagination'), one of the key-qualities he demanded from contributors to his two periodicals, *Household Words* and *All the Year Round*, and his belief in the human heart – in love, spontaneity and wonder as life's essential qualities – place Dickens solidly in the English Romantic tradition. And, perhaps most significantly, he gave his full allegiance to the most vehemently consistent of the critics of Bentham and his followers, Thomas Carlyle. Carlyle's influence on Dickens has been fully documented; and Dickens is completely – indeed proudly – open about it himself. Dedicating *Hard Times*, his most 'Carlylean' novel, to him, he wrote: 'I know it contains nothing in which you do not think with me, for no man knows your books better than I.' In July 1851, eight years before writing *A Tale of Two Cities*, the other novel in which Carlyle's influence is most obvious, he wrote to his future bio-grapher, John Forster, that he was reading 'that wonder-ful book', *The French Revolution*, 'for the 500th time'.

Forster gives his authority for Carlyle's increasing influence on Dickens: 'there was no one whom in later life he honoured so much, or had a more profound regard for'. By the time he wrote *Bleak House*, Dickens had certainly read most of Carlyle's major writings; he was particularly influenced by *Chartism* (1840) and *Past and Present* (1843).

What Dickens shared with Carlyle was a hatred of Bentham's doctrine of utility and its social and economic consequences. Contribution to 'the greatest happiness of the greatest number' as the criterion of good, Bentham's most famous dictum, sounded benevolent; but, for Dickens, as for Carlyle, it was the opposite: calculated, determinist, mechanistic. For them, Bentham's followers, the Utilitarians, reduced all relationships to self-interest; and worse, to what Carlyle branded in *Past and Present* as 'Cash-payment', the 'cash-nexus'. The main economic consequence of Utilitarianism was *laissez-faire* economics, a wages system based on statistics and controlled solely by the market: a system, with the near-poverty it brought to many, repugnant to both Dickens and Carlyle. For William Hazlitt, in *The Spirit of the Age* (1825), Bentham, with all his zeal to systematize and reform the law, had reduced the mind of man 'to a machine'; in his own way, Dickens weighed against the human consequences of that as consistently as did Carlyle. The philosophical formulations were Carlyle's; but a great many of them only confirmed Dickens's own instinctive convictions.

Eight years before writing *Bleak House*, Dickens had come nearest to specific anti-Benthamite criticism in his caricature of the statistician Mr Filer in *The Chimes*, his second Christmas Book. Utilitarian statistics in their coldness and destruction of life, imaged in Thomas Gradgrind, would again be the main target of his most 'philosophical' novel, *Hard Times*. *Dombey and Son* gives us a powerful picture of the 'cash-nexus', of the alienating and destructive power of money, focused in Dombey himself, but percolating through a whole society. In *Bleak House* it is the *total* setting – the web of Chancery, the horrors of the London slums, the perversions of government, philanthropy and religion – that exemplifies even more strongly what Dickens detested: self-interest as the only calculus, and the corruption and blindness that follow from it.

In *Dombey and Son*, the symbol of the new way of life which, as Kathleen Tillotson puts it in *Novels of the Eighteen-Forties* (1954), 'links high and low', is the railway. There is some ambiguity in our response to it – as there was no doubt in Dickens – excitement as well as fear. The symbol that links high and low in *Bleak House* is infectious disease. Here there can be no possible ambiguity in our response and the difference is one of the things that makes *Bleak House* the first of Dickens's great 'dark' novels.

What makes this darkness so pervasive is that Dickens, like Carlyle, offers no coherent alternative to the condition-of-England they both so hated. Religion, one obvious 'alternative', meant the 'Dandy' Puseyites, or the Evangelicals of Exeter Hall, or unctuous hypocrites like the Rev. Mr Chadband – or, worst of all, the oppressive Puritans like Miss Barbary. In politics the choice seemed to be between the Dandies again, the Coodles and Doodles, 'the Governing Class who do not govern' – as Carlyle called them in *Past and Present* – and, at the opposite extreme, Chartism, the working-class movement which, between 1837 and 1848, had campaigned, with threats of physical violence, for the People's Charter: a Parliament made truly representative by universal suffrage, vote by secret ballot, abolition of the property qualification and annually elected Parliaments. Dickens, however, was too suspicious of Parliament itself, and too frightened of 'the mob', ever to support the Chartists. The sudden terrifying sight of an armed, pillaging mob at night, in the industrial Midlands, as seen by Little Nell and her grandfather, in *The Old Curiosity Shop*, followed by the Gordon Riots (1780) of *Barnaby Rudge*, sufficiently show Dickens's fear of mob-violence in the 1840s. He makes it abundantly clear in letters and speeches that he never supported 'physical force Chartism', whatever his sympathy for the People's Charter itself. In his 'Postscript' to *Our Mutual Friend*, defending his view of the Poor Law, he shows that he placed his trust in 'the common sense and senses of common people', rather than in political parties or doctrines. This unpolitical, unphilosophical creed – 'sentimental radicalism' Walter Bagehot called it – is the interpretation of Dickens's social attitudes given by George Orwell: 'certainly a subversive writer', he wrote of him; 'a radical, one might truthfully say a rebel'; but 'in the ordinarily accepted sense of the word . . . not a "revolutionary" writer' ('Charles Dickens', 1939).

The most startling event in *Bleak House*, 'Chancellor' Krook's death by spontaneous combustion, has been seen as a symbolic 'revolutionary' act: the wished-for self-destruction of a corrupt institution. It is inescapably that. But it is something else too. As Michael Goldberg stresses in *Carlyle and Dickens* (1972), the imagery surrounding it is apocalyptic: the chapter-title, 'The Appointed Time', suggests the Last Judgment. Miss Flite is even more explicit:

I expect a judgment. Shortly. On the Day of Judgment. I have discovered that the sixth seal mentioned in the Revelations is the Great Seal. It has been open a long time!   (ch. 3).

The reference is to the earth's destruction and God's punishment of the rich and mighty. It is a warning of divine vengeance to come; just as Carlyle portrayed the fire of the French Revolution. But the violence of the Revolution was a fact; the symbolic act here, the divine vengeance on Chancery and on all the corruptions of the world of *Bleak House*, is, as Goldberg claims, an alternative to human revolutionary violence: imagined by a man who may have been excited by the liberating force of violence, but who ultimately feared and hated it.

Chapter 2

Bleak House: the novel

Structure: the double narrative

The main plot of *Bleak House* – the discovery of her parentage by the illegitimate Esther Summerson – was the most complicated Dickens had by then written – perhaps the most complicated he ever wrote. Its ramifications seem endless and embrace most of the novel's chief characters. But it is only one of a number of plots. There is the story of Esther's own progress, as John Jarndyce's ward, to her eventual marriage with Dr Allan Woodcourt: a progress marred physically by her disfigurement from small-pox, and psychologically by her inability to believe that Woodcourt is in love with her and her consequent acceptance of Jarndyce's proposal of marriage. There is the story of the two wards of Court, also looked after by John Jarndyce: Ada Clare, Esther's 'darling', and her cousin Richard Carstone; of their falling in love with each other and marrying; and of Richard's deterioration and early death. There is the murder of the lawyer Tulkinghorn, the false accusations as to its perpetrator, and Inspector Bucket's eventual arrest of Mlle Hortense. There is Caddy Jellyby's progress from her wretched life as her mother's ink-stained amanuensis to her happy marriage – and career – with Prince Turveydrop. And there is the restoration of Trooper George to *his* mother, the old and loving housekeeper at Chesney Wold: an ironical comment on the grim ending of the main plot, Esther's discovery of her mother dead at the entrance to the paupers' graveyard, where her lover lies buried. But enveloping all these plots is the equally grim story of the Chancery case of Jarndyce and Jarndyce that only ends in ch. 65, two chapters from the end of the novel, when the whole of the estate at issue is discovered to have been swallowed up in legal costs.

Bleak House, then, is remarkably dense in both plot and character. It required the greatest creative gifts to shape such diversified life into a unity. Its very density led many contemporary critics to deny its great advance in structure in Dickens's work: it suffered from 'an absolute want of construction', wrote the *Spectator*. But Dickens's friend and biographer, John Forster, thought it perhaps the best piece of construction in all his work. T. S. Eliot has echoed his praise. Eliot was most impressed by Dickens's anticipation of the Wilkie Collins detective story; Forster by his much wider-ranging structural powers: 'Nothing', he says, 'is introduced at random, everything tends to the catastrophe, the various lines of the plot converge and fit to its centre.' To keep such control as that implies was, of course, made immensely difficult by the monthly part serial system agreed on by Dickens and his publishers; Dickens's own notes, written in advance for each monthly part, show how he used such a challenge for the effects he intended. Suspense, the intensification of theme, the comment implied by an ironical juxtaposition, could all be achieved and heightened by the skilful use of the monthly part.

If *Bleak House* stands, chronologically, at the centre of Dickens's writing-career, its advances in structure give it the status of a landmark. Formally, it marks the final abandonment of the picaresque, the genre that had given Dickens his immense early popularity. Instead of the wanderings of his early heroes, Pickwick or Oliver or Nicholas Nickleby, we have an intense focus on London and, within London, on the all-pervading legal world of the Court of Chancery: presented as corrupt and life-destroying, a ghastly parody of a Court founded to administer justice and equity. It is a world that includes the novel's central and terrible slum, Tom-all-Alone's, since 'this desirable property is in Chancery, of course' (ch. 16): the subject of an interminable law-suit like the case of Jarndyce and Jarndyce that dominates the novel. England, outside London, is compressed into virtually only three houses and some hovels: Chesney Wold, the Dedlocks' 'place' in Lincolnshire; Boythorn's old 'parsonage house' nearby; Bleak House itself, near St Alban's; and, within walking distance of it, the brickmakers' hovels. All of these, except Boythorn's home, are given deliberate links with Chancery. Chesney Wold, with its houseparties, is one centre of the fashionable world; and, as the novel's two deliberately juxtaposed opening chapters, 'In Chancery' and 'In Fashion', make clear, the world of fashion 'is not so unlike the Court of Chancery, but that we may pass from the one scene to the other, as the crow flies' (ch. 2) – and as the novel itself repeatedly does. Bleak House, John Jarndyce's home, was given that new name in its decay, after his great-uncle, old Tom Jarndyce, a victim of Jarndyce and Jarndyce, the 'family curse', had shot himself – appropriately enough, in a public house just off London's Chancery Lane. The brickmakers' battered wives, and Jo, the crossing-sweeper, tramp often enough between the St Alban's hovels and Tom-all-Alone's to make the link only too clear. Only Boythorn's home and the 'iron country' in the north, where Mr Rouncewell, son of the housekeeper of Chesney Wold, has made his fortune, are free of Chancery; and the contrast is deliberately intended.

The all-pervasiveness of the corrupt world of Chancery is, then, central to the novel's structure. It is the first of Dickens's 'systems', with its own language – or languages

– and its own symbols. The empty rhetoric of 'Conversation' Kenge, one of Chancery's successful practitioners, sums up one aspect of it:

We are a prosperous community, Mr Jarndyce, a very prosperous community. We are a great country, Mr Jarndyce, we are a very great country. This is a great system, Mr Jarndyce, and would you wish a great country to have a little system? Now, really, really!'

He said this at the stair-head, gently moving his right hand as if it were a silver trowel, with which to spread the cement of his words on the structure of the system, and consolidate it for a thousand ages.   (ch. 62)

The secrecy and love of power of the 'eminent solicitor', Mr Tulkinghorn, 'high priest of noble mysteries', buttoned up in his rusty clothes, sums up another aspect. Chancery's major symbol is the fog that dominates the first chapter and only lifts in the last. But other elements – the excessive heat of the Inns of Court in the long vacation, the dust that covers everything in Tulkinghorn's chambers, the close, 'steaming' night that begins 'the Appointed Time', the chapter that ends with Krook's Spontaneous Combustion – all these skilfully evoke the world of Chancery too.

The creation of so powerful and sinister a system at the centre of the novel is a major structural advance by Dickens; its rendering through symbol, language and atmosphere one of his major achievements. But it must not crowd out two equally bold advances in structure: a much greater use of discontinuous narrative, switching between apparently unconnected characters and events; and – a complete and even bolder innovation – the use of two juxtaposed narratives: the impersonal, detached narrator's in the present tense; and Esther Summerson's, the involved heroine's, in the past, recording events that had happened several years earlier.

Discontinuous narrative as a formal device anticipates much twentieth-century writing. Dickens uses it quite consciously for his own ends: to show the ultimate connectedness of the apparently unconnected. The inter-connectedness Dickens achieves in *Bleak House*, the bringing together of many seemingly disparate plots and a host of disparate characters – the powerful sense, above all, that there is no escape from such interconnexion, that 'no man is an island', however high or low in the social scale – is the true, encompassing theme of *Bleak House*. And, through his controlled use of a switching narrative, Dickens constantly keeps it before us:

What connexion can there be, between the place in Lincolnshire, the house in town, the Mercury in power, and the whereabout of Jo the outlaw with the broom, who had that distant ray of light upon him when he swept the churchyard step? What connexion can there have been between many people in the innumerable histories of this world, who, from opposite sides of great gulfs, have, nevertheless, been very curiously brought together!   (ch. 16)

Through the alternation, throughout the novel, of two narratives – the third-person narrator's and Esther Summerson's – Dickens achieves something new. We can see it, with Morton Zabel (introduction to the Riverside Edition of *Bleak House*, 1956), as 'a depth of focus, a third dimension in his perspective'. Or we can see it as a strategy for juxtaposing the most strongly contrasted points of view. That of the third-person narrator is impersonal, detached; but it has behind it Dickens's own indignation with mid-nineteenth-century English society, character-ized as both Chancery and the world of fashion. Its tone can vary greatly. It can be savagely satirical, as in the many descriptions of the Chancery world or in the great set-scenes: Nemo's death and burial; Krook's Spontaneous Combustion; Jo's death. It can deploy a quiet, but generally deadly irony, as in the treatment of Tulkinghorn. Or it can ring all the changes in comic effect of the earlier Dickens: from the egregious Chadband to the sympathetic comedy of the Bagnets. Much of the new power of *Bleak House* comes from this mastery of the third-person narrator's variety of tone.

The structure of Esther's first-person narrative is quite different: personal and continuous as against impersonal and discontinuous. It is the record of her own self-discovery (both literal and psychological) and her eventual salvation through marriage to Allan Woodcourt. Much of her story is of suffering: of her guilt-tormented childhood; her illness and disfigurement; her mistake in not seeing Woodcourt's love for her. Its tone varies little: it is uniformly delicate, self-disparaging, often painfully hypersensitive. Her first words set this tone: 'I have a great difficulty in beginning to write my portion of these pages, for I know I am not clever. I always knew that' (ch. 3, 'A Progress'). In fact, there is an obvious if subtle irony in Dickens's attitude towards Esther from the start. He gives her great instinctive intelligence and a quick sensibility. Her judgments of people and events are almost invariably right. As narrator, she quietly but firmly registers Dickens's own criticism of the corrupt Chancery world about her. And the fact that she does this from *within*, with the authority of the past tense, as against the external, immediate criticism of the third-person narrator, indicates how much the novel gains from the double narrative.

To make Esther the narrator of half the novel was a bold experiment; it was also a difficult one. To enter fully and imaginatively into the consciousness of an emotionally deprived child and young woman, excessively shy, submissive and modest – as Jane Austen had entered into Fanny Price in *Mansfield Park* and Charlotte Brontë into

Lucy Snowe in *Villette* – was, for Dickens (for any male novelist), an even greater challenge. And, from the beginning, he was criticised for it. A 'difficult enterprise, full of hazard in any case, not worth success, and certainly not successful', wrote Forster in his *Life of Dickens*. Charlotte Brontë was much sharper on Esther herself: 'too often weak and twaddling'; 'an amiable nature is caricatured, not faithfully rendered'.

Criticism of Esther has continued. For Angus Wilson, in his centenary study, *The World of Dickens*, 1970, Esther's character is the novel's 'central defect'; above all, her 'reporting to us, with an almost intolerable coyness, all the praises that others give her'. It is difficult at times not to dislike her sentimentality, her passiveness, her self-disparagement, her predictability. Her goodness seems *too* absolute. Above all, she has all the characteristics of the Victorian 'womanly woman': the dedication to her housekeeping keys; the constant sobbing, with joy or sorrow; the apparent enjoyment of all her middle-aged and de-sexing nicknames ('Old Mother Hubbard' and the rest).

But it is essential – as with any novel – to remember the novelist's 'point of view'. Esther is deliberately subjective, deliberately absolute. Formally, the alternation of the double narrative compels her to be so: her subjectivity is the opposite swing of the pendulum from the omniscient, detached, confident voice of the impersonal narrator. And, psychologically, she is presented from the inside: the first of Dickens's heroines to be so. Q. D. Leavis, one of her strongest defenders, has stressed how accurate and acute a pre-Freudian study of an emotionally starved, illegitimate young woman Esther is; particularly in her self-abnegation, self-criticism, need of others' good opinion, and fear of sexuality. Such a person must constantly assuage her 'guilt', commit acts of exaggerated self-sacrifice. Many details dramatize such a portrait; two, in particular, stand out: her burying her 'dear old doll' (her only childhood-companion) under a tree, when she leaves her aunt's home (ch. 3); and, much later, as a young woman, her burning the flowers Allan Woodcourt had given her many months before, after laying them for a moment on Ada's lips, on her acceptance of Jarndyce's proposal of marriage (ch. 44). In a brilliant stroke of insight, Dickens makes Esther return to the buried doll after her rejection of Mr Guppy's clumsy proposal:

I . . . felt as if an old chord had been more coarsely touched than it ever had been since the days of the dear old doll, long buried in the garden. (ch. 9)

Dickens clearly attempts – and often attains – a new depth of focus by his switching of points of view between the two narrators; and this is helped by obviously intended juxtapositions and deliberate overlaps between the two. Examples are the beginnings of chs. 52 and 57, where we are given Esther's responses to major events – Tulkinghorn's murder and Lady Dedlock's flight – which have already been described by the third-person narrator. This points to a greater contrast, maintained throughout the novel, between events in time, the onward thrust of the several plots, as told (however differently) by both narrators, and the static – or timeless – descriptions. These descriptions communicate the novel's particular and powerful atmosphere; and, in addition, they have something of the force of musical *leitmotifs*, both suggestive and interconnecting. Two of them, the novel's brilliant opening, describing the London fog, and the no less impressive picture in ch. 2 of Chesney Wold, virtually afloat in the rain, will be analysed in the next section (pp. 33–5).

Chancery itself is constantly described: by John

Jarndyce, who refuses to enter its portals; and by its disillusioned victims, poor crazed little Miss Flite, Gridley, and – before succumbing to its lure – by Richard Carstone. If, formally, like the London fog, it is static and timeless, in substance it exerts a sinister influence over all who come into contact with it. John Jarndyce's passionate warning to Richard against putting any trust in the case of Jarndyce and Jarndyce sufficiently shows his fear of it:

'Rick, Rick!' cried my guardian, with a sudden terror in his manner, and in an altered voice, and putting up his hands as if he would have stopped his ears, 'for the love of God, don't found a hope or expectation on the family curse!   (ch. 24)

Miss Flite's image of the magnet, to explain the Court's horrible fascination, gives it an almost supernatural power:

'It's the Mace and Seal upon the table.' What could they do, did she think? I mildly asked her.
'Draw,' returned Miss Flite. 'Draw people on, my dear. Draw peace out of them. Sense out of them. Good looks out of them. Good qualities out of them. I have felt them even drawing my rest away in the night. Cold and glittering devils!'
                                                                    (ch. 35)

Such passages *frame* the plot, give the narrative of Richard's deterioration under the spell of Chancery its inevitability.

Descriptions of Chesney Wold act as a similar framing device to the main plot of Esther's discovery that Lady Dedlock is her mother. They show Dickens's art – an art manifested throughout *Bleak House* – of making place intimately reflect consciousness. Esther's first view of Chesney Wold is entirely innocent of the secret it holds for her. It is simply 'a picturesque old house, in a fine park richly wooded'; beautiful and benign: 'O, the solemn woods over which the light and shadow travelled swiftly, as if Heavenly wings were sweeping on benignant errands through the summer air.' Her main impression is of 'the serene and peaceful flush that rested on all around it' and of its 'undisturbed repose' (ch. 18).

Many chapters later, when her mother has just told her the secret of her illegitimate birth, Esther describes the house again: instead of lying in the 'complete repose' of her first description (she makes the interlocking and ironical point herself), it 'now looked like the obdurate and unpitying watcher of my mother's misery'. Its once impressive Gothic features are now only sinister and frightening; and, with acute psychological understanding, Dickens makes Esther herself take on her mother's guilt:

my echoing footsteps brought it suddenly into my mind that there was a dreadful truth in the legend of the Ghost's Walk; that it was I, who was to bring calamity upon the stately house; and that my warning feet were haunting it even then.

(ch. 36)

A final description of the house and park at the end of the novel frames more than Esther's and her mother's plot. It frames both the Dedlocks, the scandal and their tragedy, and the kind of life they have lived; it is the end of one world of experience:

A labyrinth of grandeur, less the property of an old family of human beings and their ghostly likenesses, than of an old family of echoings and thunderings which start out of their hundred graves at every sound, and go resounding through the building . . .

Thus Chesney Wold. With so much of itself abandoned to darkness and vacancy; with so little change under the summer shining or the wintry lowering; so sombre and motionless always . . . – passion and pride, even to the stranger's eye, have died away from the place in Lincolnshire, and yielded it to dull repose.   (ch. 66)

That description follows a passage of pure satire of Volumnia at her annual county ball; but it is anything but satirical itself. Its mixture of tones – of pathos and sombreness, as well as ironical awareness – reflects a similar rich blend in one whole strand of the narrative that it both encapsulates and concludes.

Dickens employs a further important structural device to underline the irrevocableness of the novel's main catastrophe, Lady Dedlock's disgrace and flight: the evocation of a sense of Fate through the creation of omens and through a pervasive use of irony. (The irony deserves a section to itself: see pp. 68–76.) The omens are used in a remarkably Shakespearean way; and it is striking how many Shakespeare quotations and allusions there are throughout the novel – the great majority of them from the tragedies.

The most obvious omen is the Ghost's Walk at Chesney Wold. It is the title of an early chapter – ch. 7 – and the housekeeper's telling of the story that gave the terrace its name leaves no doubt of its significance now: 'I will walk here, until the pride of this house is humbled', says the crippled seventeenth-century Lady Dedlock. 'And when calamity, or when disgrace is coming to it, let the Dedlocks listen to my step!' It is an omen we are never allowed to forget. At the end of the scene in which the disguised Lady Dedlock has made Jo take her to the squalid places associated with her lover's death, the sound is particularly loud: 'in all these years', says Mrs. Rouncewell, 'I never heard the step, upon the Ghost's Walk, more distinct than it is to-night!' (ch. 16). By the end of the novel, when Lady Dedlock has left her letter of confession and flown from the London house, the housekeeper simply uses the Ghost's Walk to state the truth:

When I saw my Lady yesterday, George, she looked to me – and I may say at me too – as if the steps on the Ghost's Walk had almost walked her down. . . . It's going on for sixty years that I have been in this family, and I never had any fear for it before. But it's breaking up, my dear; the great old Dedlock family is breaking up . . . the step on the Ghost's Walk will walk my Lady down, George; it has been many a day behind her, and now it will pass her, and go on.   (ch. 58)

As in many of his novels, Dickens uses paintings – as Hogarth had done in his engravings – to give an ironical underlining to his meaning. The frozen Dedlock portraits, in their state dress, underscore the stranglehold of the past on the Dedlock household. But the treatment of Lady Dedlock's own portrait makes it much more of an omen than these. The clear cold sunshine, as Sir Leicester and his wife return to Chesney Wold from Paris, 'touches the ancestral portraits with bars and patches of brightness, never contemplated by the painters'; but 'Athwart the picture of my Lady, over the great chimney-piece, it throws a broad bend-sinister of light that strikes down crookedly into the hearth, and seems to rend it' (ch. 12).

Later in the novel, the shadow on Lady Dedlock's portrait is made even more disturbing: 'At this hour and by this light it changes into threatening hands raised up, and menacing the handsome face with every breath that stirs' (ch. 40). Phiz's illustration, *Sunset in the Long Drawing-Room at Chesney Wold*, shows the shadow moving menacingly upwards.

If omens and the shadows on paintings suggest a hidden Fate at work, secrecy is woven into the very structure of the novel. *Bleak House* has been called a 'social detective-story', 'a story of mystery'; but the best description of Dickens's way of telling it is Percy Lubbock's, in his classical book on the form of the novel, *The Craft of Fiction* (1921). 'Labyrinthine mystification' is the phrase he offers; and it points not only to the ramifications of the main plot – and indeed to the multiplicity of the plots – but, beyond that, to mysteries and secrecies below the plot, inherent in *all* human experience, which *Bleak House* constantly suggests. The use of the double narrative undoubtedly contributes to this deliberately implied opaqueness: consciousness of the unfolding of events is sometimes given to one narrator, sometimes to the other; at times the full significance of the events seems hidden from both; at other times – as in the final catastrophe of Lady Dedlock's death – full revelation is given to all (including the reader), and light floods back on all the obscured past.

But, beyond even the demands of the plot, secrecy is an integral part of the life and language of the whole world of Chancery. It is natural to all the lawyers: to Tulkinghorn, legal adviser to Sir Leicester Dedlock and to many of the peerage; to Vholes, in his cat-and-mouse dealings with Richard Carstone; to Guppy, the solicitor's clerk, in his ferreting out of Lady Dedlock's secret. In Krook, the illiterate parody-Chancellor, and in the money-grubbing Grandfather Smallweed, secrecy is combined with intense suspicion. As it is in Mrs Snagsby, whose suspicious pursuit of her innocent husband, unwittingly forced into a web of secrets, is a clear parody of the secretive machinations of the legal world.

But it is Tulkinghorn who, above all, epitomizes the secret world that is the essence of *Bleak House*. Almost every metaphor and image in the first telling description of him in ch. 2 plays its part in creating this effect. 'He is surrounded by a mysterious halo of family confidences; of which he is known to be the silent depositor.' 'Mute, close, irresponsive to any glancing light, his dress is like himself.' Later, he is 'an Oyster of the old school, whom nobody can open'. But, as well as secrecy, Tulkinghorn embodies power; and the particular kind of power he has – and its source – Dickens makes unerringly clear through language: both Tulkinghorn's own language, in its deliberate low key, and the language used by the third-person narrator to describe him. It is the power of 'ultimate spiritual nullity' (the phrase is P. J. M. Scott's): absolute in its blindness to all human feeling and totally reductive. This reductiveness we see in the first picture of Tulkinghorn at work in his chambers:

> He has some manuscript near him, but is not referring to it. With the round top of an inkstand, and two broken bits of sealing-wax, he is silently and slowly working out whatever train of indecision is in his mind. Now, the inkstand top is in the middle: now, the red bit of sealing-wax, now the black bit.
> (ch. 10)

The inkstand, the sealing-wax, are clearly clients' lives, which are all reduced to things.

Small physical details make the same point. After his triumphant set-scene, in which he tells the assembled guests at Chesney Wold his 'story' (the past history of Lady Dedlock, which will ruin her), Tulkinghorn makes no concession to feeling whatever: either his own or Lady Dedlock's. Instead:

> Perhaps there is a rather increased sense of power upon him, as he loosely grips one of his veinous wrists with his other hand, and holding it behind his back walks noiselessly up and down.
> (ch. 16)

But his own language makes the point clearer still. When Lady Dedlock speaks to him of 'my secret', Tulkinghorn at once contradicts her: 'It is no longer your secret. Excuse me. That is just the mistake. It is my secret in trust for Sir Leicester and the family.' The motive here might seem to be loyalty to Sir Leicester; but the language points to something else. The legal phrase is again reductive: to Tulkinghorn, Lady Dedlock's past, with all the feelings it once had, is simply a piece of family property – a piece of red or black sealing-wax to be manipulated to its right position.

Spiritual nullity needs little more in the way of human motive; if Tulkinghorn is faithful to Sir Leicester, he is, as Lady Dedlock tells Esther – explaining his remorselessness in tracking her down – 'mechanically faithful without attachment'. He has virtually only two forms of language: that of suppressed power, in which he exposes Lady Dedlock at Chesney Wold, or threatens Mlle Hortense with prison, or quietly, even courteously, forces Lady Dedlock to listen to him; and something nearer to a kind of 'non-language', a refusal to commit himself, as when he 'buries' salutations or hides any views he may have: 'It is a part of Mr Tulkinghorn's policy and mastery to have no political opinions; indeed, *no* opinions.'

Two incidents throw the Tulkinghorn way of life (were it not for its power, his death-in-life) into relief: the apparently casual reference to the suicide of his one bachelor friend, 'a man of the same mould and a lawyer too'; and the grotesque account of his own funeral. Both have a Dostoevskian power (one understands Dostoevsky's great admiration for Dickens: see pp. 95–6). The friend lived the same kind of life as Tulkinghorn 'until he was seventy-five years old, and then, suddenly conceiving (as it is supposed) an impression that it was too monotonous, gave his gold watch to his hairdresser one Summer evening and walked leisurely home to the Temple, and hanged himself' (ch. 22). Tulkinghorn's own funeral, in Lincoln's Inn Fields, in its excessive parade of formal mourning ('The Peerage contributes more four-wheeled affliction than has ever been seen in that neighbourhood') and total lack of feeling, is a kind of comic revenge on his life (ch. 53).

Tulkinghorn is a true landmark in Dickens's perception of the destructive power of nullity. He is followed by similarly impressive creations: by the financier, Merdle, of *Little Dorrit* and by the powerful lawyer, Jaggers, of *Great*

Expectations. But Tulkinghorn is much more conscious of what he is doing than Merdle; more sinister, in his inscrutability, than Jaggers.

Secrecy and the sense of Fate are, then, central to the atmosphere of *Bleak House*; they pervade plot and character and language alike; we are never allowed to forget them. And Dickens cannot resist parodying them too. The main victims of this comic parody are the mild, timid law-stationer, Mr Snagsby, and his shrewish, suspicious wife. Mrs Snagsby's growing suspicions of her husband, culminating in the extraordinary belief that, since Snagsby befriends him, Jo must be his illegitimate son (she knows it 'as well as if a trumpet had spoken it') are clearly a grotesque parody of the Lady Dedlock–Esther plot and of Tulkinghorn's pursuit. Even the language is echoed:

And into whatsoever atmosphere of secrecy his own shadow may pass, let all concerned in the secrecy beware! For the watchful Mrs Snagsby is there too – bone of his bone, flesh of his flesh, shadow of his shadow.   (ch. 25)

A pawn in Tulkinghorn's machinations, Snagsby finds himself 'wrapped round with secrecy and mystery', till his life is a burden to him. When Guppy's friend, Tony Jobling (*alias* Weevle), takes over the room at Krook's house in which the law-writer 'Nemo' had died, Snagsby invokes, in his own way, the concept of Fate:

'It's a curious coincidence, as you say,' answers Weevle, once more glancing up and down the court.
  'Seems a Fate in it, don't there?' suggests the stationer.
  'There does.'
  'Just so,' observes the stationer, with his confirmatory cough. 'Quite a Fate in it. Quite a Fate.'   (ch. 32)

Earlier, Snagsby has been at the centre of one of the novel's funniest scenes: Chadband's sermon on the subject of the extremely reluctant Jo. Mention of 'the unnatural parents of this slumbering Heathen' (Jo is now asleep) 'accidentally finishes' Snagsby and reduces his wife to hysterics. From then on the pursuit gathers pace: Snagsby begins, 'go where he will, to be attended by another shadow than his own, hardly less constant than his own, hardly less quiet than his own'. Mrs. Snagsby, a 'ghostly shade, frilled and night-capped', is as inexorable in her half-comic way, as Tulkinghorn or even Inspector Bucket are in theirs.

In a novel as permeated with Shakespeare as *Bleak House*, Dickens, in creating such a parody, was, in his own way, following Shakespeare's favourite device – paramount above all in the so-called 'problem-plays' – of creating a low-world comic sub-plot to echo or ironically twist the serious plots and themes of the play's main protagonists. And the effect in both Shakespeare and Dickens is much the same: the parody both intensifies the main plot and, by comically framing it, forces us to ask questions about its ultimate importance.

Language

Symbolism

The new density of plot and characters in *Bleak House* demanded a new range of language. Dickens shows equal assurance in a great variety of effects: in descriptions, melodrama, psychological exploration, the build-up of irony. Vitality is evident everywhere; and with it, an imaginative boldness that takes many different forms. Dickens never forgets the declaration in his Preface: 'I have purposely dwelt on the romantic side of familiar things.' The context of that may have been his defence of Krook's Spontaneous Combustion, where the 'romantic' is taken to an extreme; but again and again the seemingly familiar is given an extra dimension of meaning, almost

always through a skilful use of symbols. The shadows
darkening Lady Dedlock's portrait in Chesney Wold
become omens; the flagged terrace pavement becomes the
Ghost's Walk, with all its implications for the Dedlock
family.

The two probably best-known descriptions in the novel
are of natural phenomena familiar enough: the London
fog of the opening chapter and the effect of the rain on
Chesney Wold in ch. 2. But both are treated with a
fanciful wit and a symbolic extension of meaning that give
them a much more than 'familiar' significance. Here are
the two passages:

LONDON. Michaelmas Term lately over, and the Lord
Chancellor sitting in Lincoln's Inn Hall. Implacable November
weather. As much mud in the streets, as if the waters had but
newly retired from the face of the earth, and it would not be
wonderful to meet a Megalosaurus, forty feet long or so,
waddling like an elephantine lizard up Holborn Hill. Smoke
lowering down from chimney-pots, making a soft black drizzle,
with flakes of soot in it as big as full-grown snow-flakes – gone
into mourning, one might imagine, for the death of the sun.
Dogs, undistinguishable in mire. Horses, scarcely better;
splashed to their very blinkers. Foot passengers, jostling one
another's umbrellas, in a general infection of ill-temper, and
losing their foot-hold at street-corners, where tens of thousands
of other foot passengers have been slipping and sliding since the
day broke (if this day ever broke), adding new deposits to the
crust upon crust of mud, sticking at those points tenaciously to
the pavement, and accumulating at compound interest.

Fog everywhere. Fog up the river, where it flows among
green aits and meadows; fog down the river, where it rolls
defiled among the tiers of shipping, and the waterside pollutions of a great (and dirty) city. Fog on the Essex marshes, fog
on the Kentish heights. Fog creeping into the cabooses of
collier-brigs, fog lying out on the yards, and hovering in the
rigging of great ships; fog drooping on the gunwales of barges
and small boats. Fog in the eyes and throats of ancient
Greenwich pensioners, wheezing by the firesides of their wards;
fog in the stem and bowl of the afternoon pipe of the wrathful

skipper, down in his close cabin; fog cruelly pinching the toes and fingers of his shivering little 'prentice boy on deck. Chance people on the bridges peeping over the parapets into a nether sky of fog, with fog all round them, as if they were up in a balloon, and hanging in the misty clouds.

The waters are out in Lincolnshire. An arch of the bridge in the park has been sapped and sopped away. The adjacent low-lying ground, for half a mile in breadth, is a stagnant river, with melancholy trees for islands in it, and a surface punctured all over, all day long, with falling rain. My Lady Dedlock's 'place' has been extremely dreary. The weather, for many a day and night, has been so wet that the trees seem wet through, and the soft loppings and prunings of the woodman's axe can make no crash or crackle as they fall. The deer, looking soaked, leave quagmires, where they pass. The shot of a rifle loses its sharpness in the moist air, and its smoke moves in a tardy little cloud towards the green rise, coppice-topped, that makes a background for the falling rain. The view from my Lady Dedlock's own windows is alternately a lead-coloured view, and a view in Indian ink. The vases on the stone terrace in the foreground catch the rain all day; and the heavy drops fall, drip, drip, drip, upon the broad flagged pavement, called, from old time, the Ghost's Walk, all night. On Sundays, the little church in the park is mouldy; the oaken pulpit breaks out into a cold sweat; and there is a general smell and taste as of the ancient Dedlocks in their graves.

The symbolic strength of both passages is striking. The fog *is* Chancery, in all its muddle and murk and obscurantism (the fantastic Megalosaurus makes its witty point); it is also the blindness that afflicts so many of the novel's characters, a blindness that isolates and deadens them. Likewise, the rain and its aftermath of mouldiness perfectly reflect the deadness both of Chesney Wold, the ancient Dedlock estate (the Dedlock name is, of course, self-revealing) and of the world of fashion that both idolizes and bores Lady Dedlock. But, as often in Dickens, the symbol never exhausts the observation that has helped to create its relevance. Fog and rain exist here in their own right too; and we are most struck by the

imaginative energy that pursues the swirling fog into
every crevice of urban London and dockland and into the
eyes and throats of their inhabitants, and the rain and
mould into every corner of the Chesney Wold estate. But
if the effects are similar, the linguistic techniques to attain
them are very different. Both the immediacy and the
timelessness of the first passage are created largely by the
accumulated present participles: the Chancellor is sitting
and will *always* be sitting, just as the smoke will always be
lowering down and the fog always creeping and hovering.
The effects of the second passage are as much aural as
visual: the rain has reduced everything on the estate to a
silence as of death; Dickens has made the absence of
expected noises the absence of life itself.

A much more extended mingling of effects – of lyricism,
irony, as well as symbolism (here, nearer to allegory) –
saves another key-passage, the account of Tulkinghorn's
murder in ch. 48, from being merely melodramatic. In its
complex mixture – as against the pure 'Gothic' horror of
Krook's Spontaneous Combustion – it is, linguistically,
perhaps the most ambitious piece of sustained descriptive
writing in the novel; and it is worth giving virtually in full:

not only is it a still night in gardens and in woods, and on the
river where the water-meadows are fresh and green, and the
stream sparkles on among pleasant islands, murmuring weirs,
and whispering rushes; not only does the stillness attend it as it
flows where houses cluster thick, where many bridges are
reflected in it, where wharves and shipping make it black and
awful, where it winds from these disfigurements through
marshes whose grim beacons stand like skeletons washed
ashore, where it expands through the bolder region of rising
grounds, rich in corn-field, wind-mill and steeple, and where it
mingles with the ever-heaving sea; not only is it a still night on
the deep, and on the shore where the watcher stands to see the
ship with her spread wings cross the path of light that appears to
be presented to only him; but even on this stranger's wilderness
of London there is some rest . . .
What's that? Who fired a gun or pistol? Where was it? . . .

Has Mr Tulkinghorn been disturbed? His windows are dark and quiet, and his door is shut. It must be something unusual indeed, to bring him out of his shell. Nothing is heard of him, nothing is seen of him. What power of cannon might it take to shake that rusty old man out of his immovable composure?

For many years, the persistent Roman has been pointing, with no particular meaning, from that ceiling. It is not likely that he has any new meaning in him to-night. Once pointing, always pointing – like any Roman, or even Briton, with a single idea. There he is, no doubt, in his impossible attitude, pointing unavailingly, all night long. Moonlight, darkness, dawn, sunrise, day. There he is still, eagerly pointing, and no one minds him . . .

He is pointing at a table, with a bottle (nearly full of wine) and a glass upon it, and two candles that were blown out suddenly, soon after being lighted. He is pointing at an empty chair, and at a stain upon the ground before it that might be almost covered with a hand. These objects lie directly within his range. An excited imagination might suppose that there was something in them so terrific, as to drive the rest of the composition, not only the attendant big-legged boys, but the clouds and flowers and pillars too – in short the very body and soul of Allegory, and all the brains it has – stark mad. It happens surely, that every one who comes into the darkened room and looks at these things, looks up at the Roman, and that he is invested in all eyes with mystery and awe, as if he were a paralysed dumb witness.

. . . For, Mr Tulkinghorn's time is over for evermore; and the Roman pointed at the murderous hand uplifted against his life, and pointed helplessly at him, from night to morning, lying face downward on the floor, shot through the heart.

The first, obvious point to make is the use of verbal irony: the stressing of peace and quietness as a herald to the horror to come. But, as Dickens develops his picture of a still night, enriching it with images of gardens and woods, sparkling stream, and ever-heaving sea, we realise that much more is at work than irony. This is a lyrical vision in its own right: a vision of the peace that might have been, a nostalgic image of a world momentarily safe from the violence we are about to witness. All the signs of Dickens's involvement are here: the long and complex sentence of eighteen lines, beautifully controlled, that runs from 'Not only is it a still night' to 'there is some rest'; the multiplicity of view-point that moves from country-side to London and takes in houses, bridges, steeples; the move into blank verse ('where it mingles with the ever-heaving sea'), which reinforces our sense of a *poetic* organization; and, perhaps above all, that strangely moving image of the watcher on the shore standing to see the ship. But the darker world is not wholly excluded: there are the wharves and shipping that make the river 'black and awful'; and the marshes 'whose grim beacons stand like skeletons washed ashore'.

That long paragraph ends with an original and evocative image, of the stilled sounds of a distant but great city at night, now merged 'into a distant ringing hum as if the city were a vast glass, vibrating'. That change from sight to sound is all-important in the build-up of the scene, for it is an unexpected, shocking sound that shatters it.

After an ironical glance at Tulkinghorn, 'Allegory', the 'persistent Roman', ever pointing from the ceiling, takes over. We have seen him before, as an integral part of Tulkinghorn's chambers; but now Dickens's remarkable animistic power – the power to invest dumb or mechanical or even carved objects with life – gives 'the persistent Roman' an almost demonic force. He not only points, but points 'eagerly'; and what he points at (as though he had willed it) causes the people who see it to 'shriek and fly'. The Roman is clearly an emblem of Tulkinghorn's fate and at the same time powerless to prevent it: 'a paralysed dumb witness'. The brilliance of the key part he plays in the discovery of Tulkinghorn's murder points to two other of Dickens's major qualities, superbly illustrated throughout *Bleak House*: his visual imagination and his skill in infusing an all but comic effect ('the attendant big-legged boys') into a violent, highly dramatic scene. This mixture of qualities reminds us – as much of *Bleak House* does – of how Shakespearean is Dickens's genius.

Voices

As in previous novels, it is in the language of his comic or near-comic characters that Dickens's wit and fancy seem most fully engaged. All such characters give perform-ances; and, as we might well expect, such performances in *Bleak House* are remarkably vivid. Of them all, Skimpole's is the purest and the most striking, as it is the most entertaining. We know that Dickens's model was his old friend Leigh Hunt, distinguished critic and poet; and that, despite attempts, on the advice of friends, to play down external likenesses (he changed his name from Leonard to Harold and changed him from thin to fat), the original was immediately recognized. In a letter to a friend, admitting – or, rather, boasting of – what he had done ('I suppose he is the most exact portrait that ever was painted in words!'), he wrote of Skimpole: 'Of whom I will now proceed to speak as if I had only read him, and had not written him.' 'Only heard him', he should have said. For Skimpole is essentially a voice; just as Turveydrop and Chadband and, to a great extent, the solicitor's clerk, Guppy are voices too. 'Language most shows a man. Speak, that I may see thee', Ben Jonson (whom Dickens immensely admired) had written in *Discoveries*. Even without Phiz's illustrations, the voices of all four suf-ficiently reveal what Dickens wants us to know of them.

Skimpole is the quintessential aesthete: he has mastered the art of living with no responsibilities towards life or society whatever. He sketches a little, he plays the piano a little, he composes a little; but his real medium is language. He turns self-justification into an art-form;

and, in the shape and fancy and apparent water-tightness of his brilliantly specious arguments, his creator shows both enjoyment and considerable intellectual skill.

'I covet nothing', said Mr Skimpole, in the same light way, 'Possession is nothing to me. Here is my friend Jarndyce's excellent house. I feel obliged to him for possessing it. I can sketch it, and alter it. I can set it to music' (ch. 6). Dickens catches here the very timbre of fanciful 'logic' masking exploitation. And exploitation of willing victims, such as Jarndyce, is, of course, the true goal of Skimpole's charm.

'It's only you, the generous creatures, whom I envy', said Mr Skimpole . . . 'I envy you your power of doing what you do. It is what I should revel in, myself. I don't feel any vulgar gratitude to you. I almost feel as if *you* ought to be grateful to *me*, for giving you the opportunity of enjoying the luxury of generosity. I know you like it.'   (ch. 6)

'Vulgar gratitude'; 'the luxury of generosity': the capsizing of generally accepted humane values might be missed here on a quick reading; it is an integral part of the Skimpole voice.

Dickens has been criticized for the heartlessness and cynicism of Skimpole's later acts: for making him advise John Jarndyce to turn the fever-stricken Jo out of his house 'before he gets still worse' ('The amiable face with which he said it, I think I shall never forget', says Esther); for making him accept five pounds later the same night from Inspector Bucket to enable him to carry Jo away; and, later in the novel, another five pounds from Vholes to introduce Richard to him as a client to be milched. But, however heartless and cynical, these acts are not inconsistent with Skimpole's charm, nor with that persuasive voice. It is a connexion on which Dickens insists.

Shortly after his advice to turn Jo out, we are shown Skimpole entertaining himself 'by playing snatches of pathetic airs, and sometimes singing to them . . . with great expression and feeling'. Finally,

> he said he would give us a little ballad, which had come into his head, 'apropos of our young friend'; and he sang one about a Peasant boy,
>
>> 'Thrown on the wide world, doom'd to wander and roam,
>> Bereft of his parents, bereft of a home.'
>
> – quite exquisitely. It was a song that always made him cry, he told us.
>
> He was extremely gay all the rest of the evening.   (ch. 31)

Skimpole's final exit is appropriate. After his death, his Life, based on his diary, was published: 'It was considered very pleasant reading', says Esther, 'but I never read more of it myself than the sentence on which I chanced to light on opening the book. It was this. "Jarndyce, in common with most other men I have known, is the Incarnation of Selfishness."' In *Bleak House*, as elsewhere, Dickens never does things by halves.

Turveydrop is a voice too, an absurd, only just credible voice, but at its most unrestrained (and Dickens's best caricatures are always unrestrained), an extremely funny one:

> 'Where what is left among us of Deportment', he added, 'still lingers, England – alas, my country! – has degenerated very much, and is degenerating every day. She has not many gentlemen left. We are few. I see nothing to succeed us, but a race of weavers.'   (ch. 14)

'A race of weavers' is a stroke of genius; it also points to the difference between Turveydrop and Skimpole. It is exaggerated, a true conclusion to Turveydrop's absurd lament; but it is not a stage in an ultimately insidious argument. Like Skimpole, Turveydrop is an aesthete and a parasite; but a much less gifted and formidable one. Devotion to Deportment and the Prince Regent is relatively self-contained and the victims of his performance are virtually confined to his own family. But it *is* a performance – and an enjoyable one. '"For myself, my children", said Mr Turveydrop, "I am falling into the sear and yellow leaf."' The audacity of the *Macbeth* quotation shows how much he believes in his performance himself. But the point – the point that makes him part of one of the central themes of *Bleak House*, a parasite through and through – is that he takes in others too: his wife, the 'meek little dancing-mistress', who had worked herself to death for him, his son and even his daughter-in-law, Caddy Jellyby (most of the people we see with him, in fact, except Esther and the old lady at the dancing-class, who would like to bite him).

Turveydrop's stance and language, when his son Prince announces his engagement, provide one of the best smaller comic set-scenes of the novel:

'Boy,' said Mr Turveydrop, 'it is well that your sainted mother is spared this pang. Strike deep, and spare not. Strike home, sir, strike home!'   (ch. 23)

In a novel that contains so much serious rhetoric, it is characteristic of Dickens to use parody-rhetoric as a comic weapon. Turveydrop may be more of a comic than a serious monster; but at times there is an unpleasant tone to his voice too: 'But Wooman, lovely Wooman', said Mr Turveydrop, with very disagreeable gallantry [Esther is recording the scene], 'what a sex you are!' (ch. 14). And in his devotion to dress (and to little else), he anticipates the withering charge Dickens was to make against the French *ancien régime* in *A Tale of Two Cities*: 'Everybody was dressed for a Fancy Ball that was never to leave off.' Mr Turveydrop, like the French nobles, lives a life of total unreality. That is his ultimate rôle in the novel.

Chadband's is another unforgettable voice: even if we only hear it on three occasions. Chadband is one of those

Dickens grotesques who, as V. S. Pritchett has said (in *The Living Novel*, 1946), 'do not talk to one another; they talk to themselves'. A few words of edification and Chadband mesmerizes himself with his own performance. Its basis was no doubt a brand of the extreme Evangelical language that Dickens so derided. But the result – the Biblical allusions strung randomly together, the absurd repetitions, questions and answers, even the tricks of pronunciation (*untoe*, *Terewth*) – is something self-created, a unique and hilarious nonsense:

'My young friend', says Chadband, 'you are to us a pearl, you are to us a diamond, you are to us a gem, you are to us a jewel. And why, my young friend?'

'*I* don't know,' replies Jo. 'I don't know nothink.'

'My young friend', says Chadband, 'it is because you know nothing that you are to us a gem and jewel. For what are you, my young friend? Are you a beast of the field? No. A bird of the air? No. A fish of the sea or river? No. You are a human boy, my young friend. A human boy. O glorious to be a human boy!'

(ch. 19)

We have just had the scene of the policeman's threatening to take the ragged Jo, the 'human boy', into custody for not 'moving on' (the title of the chapter). We have also just seen Chadband eating 'prodigiously' at the Snagsbys' table. Chadband's absurd repetitive rhetoric may be grotesquely comic in itself; but Dickens never forgets to remind us of the reality that it hides or ignores.

Chadband's next 'sermon' is even wilder, his Biblical allusions more ridiculously mixed and out-of-place; and this time he is completely unaware of the havoc he is causing to the Snagsbys; of the suspicions his references to Jo's parents are awakening in Mrs Snagsby:

'Or put it, my juvenile friends', said Chadband . . . 'that the unnatural parents of this slumbering Heathen – for parents he had, my juvenile friends, beyond a doubt – after casting him forth to the wolves and the vultures, and the wild dogs and the young gazelles, and the serpents, went back to their dwellings and had their pipes, and their pots, and their flutings and their dancings, and their malt liquors, and their butcher's meat and poultry, would *that* be Terewth?'

Mrs Snagsby replies by delivering herself a prey to spasms.
(ch. 25)

On these first two occasions Chadband is simply a voice, intoning his nonsense on the edge of the plot. But Dickens does not allow him to get away so lightly. In ch. 54 he is one of the blackmailing quartet, led by Grandfather Smallweed, that invades Sir Leicester's library. He has the same voice; but, put to a practical, unscrupulous purpose, it has an unmistakably sinister ring to it:

Then why are we here, my friends? Air we in possession of a sinful secret, and doe we require corn, and wine, and oil – or, what is much the same thing, money – for the keeping thereof? Probably so, my friends.

Each of these three performers – Skimpole, Turveydrop, Chadband – lives in an unreal world of his own. Each uses an exaggeratedly unreal language – highly entertainingly – for his own ends. Dickens's genius, displayed for the first time so fully and variedly in *Bleak House* – and not only with these comic characters – is to show the intimate link between particular kinds of language and particular kinds of corruption. It is a highly sophisticated art of exposure.

Guppy, the cockney solicitor's clerk, is a voice too and at times a singularly ridiculous one. But he is a mixture, not a pure performer like the other three. In scenes such as the dinner with his friends Jobling and 'Chick' Smallweed, he harks back to the satire of *Sketches by Boz*. As an amateur detective, constantly ferreting out secrets, he plays a considerable part in the plot. But it is as Esther's would-be lover that his voice becomes both

memorable and absurd. A mixture of legal jargon,
cockney domesticity and romantic cliché is far from
simple to capture; Dickens does it perfectly, if cruelly:

'My own abode is lodgings at Penton Place, Pentonville. It is
lowly, but airy, open at the back, and considered one of the
'ealthiest outlets. Miss Summerson! In the mildest language, I
adore you. Would you be so kind as to allow me (as I may say)
to file a declaration – to make an offer!' Mr Guppy went down
on his knees.   (ch. 9)

The same voice has to accommodate Guppy's panic in
ch. 38 when, after Esther's disfigurement, he wants
desperately to make it clear that his offer is over. And it
does service once again, near the end of the novel, when
Guppy begs 'to lay the ouse in Walcot Square, the
business, and myself', before her. This time the antics of
his grotesque mother add to the humiliation of his
rejection. To have made Guppy Esther's unsuccessful
suitor was a disconcerting, if boldly comic, stroke.
Dickens's motive was clearly to give the ridiculous voice
he had created the most unlikely experience to founder
on.

Rhetoric

The parody-rhetoric of both Turveydrop and Chadband
has already been noted. For the comic effect to work,
there has to be a serious rhetoric to set it against; and of
this *Bleak House* has its full measure. At his most
indignant, Dickens moves naturally from description to
rhetorical apostrophe; only the imperative will suf-
ficiently express his anger. Here, as they bury Nemo, it is
invoked against London pauper graveyards:

Come night, come darkness, for you cannot come too soon, or
stay too long, by such a place as this! Come, straggling lights
into the windows of the ugly houses; and you who do iniquity
therein, do it at least with this dread scene shut out! Come,

flame of gas, burning so sullenly above the iron gate, on which
the poisoned air deposits its witch-ointment slimy to the touch!
It is well that you should call to every passer-by, 'Look here!'
                                                              (ch. 11)

The macabre detail at the end, the 'witch-ointment slimy
to the touch', adds authentic physical horror. But the
power of the passage is rhetorical: the repeated imperative
'Come!' – to night, to darkness, to straggling lights, to
flame of gas – dramatically indicates Dickens's urgency.

The two best-known apostrophes in the novel – those
that follow the deaths of Krook and Jo – will be discussed
later. But another passage, of equal urgency, shows
Dickens's rhetorical range. It is not an apostrophe, but a
daring and imaginative personifying of Tom-All-Alone's
and the contagion that such slums impart:

But [Tom] has his revenge. Even the winds are his messengers,
and they serve him in these hours of darkness. There is not a
drop of Tom's corrupted blood but propagates infection and
contagion somewhere. It shall pollute, this very night, the
choice stream (in which chemists on analysis would find the
genuine nobility) of a Norman house, and his Grace shall not be
able to say Nay to the infamous alliance. There is not an atom
of Tom's slime, not a cubic inch of any pestilential gas in which
he lives, not one obscenity or degradation about him, not an
ignorance, not a wickedness, not a brutality of his committing,
but shall work its retribution, through every order of society, up
to the proudest of the proud, and to the highest of the high.
Verily, what with tainting, plundering, and spoiling, Tom has
his revenge.   (ch. 46)

This is the central warning of the novel: the vulnerability
of a Norman Duke only rhetorically exaggerates the fates
of Esther and Lady Dedlock. The repeated 'Tom has his
revenge' frames the passage; and 'Verily', that could be
merely an archaism, adds the formality of conviction to
the repetition.

Between these two very different kinds of rhetoric – that

of social indignation and the comic rhetoric of the 'voices' – there is a third, quite different again: the natural speaking voice of a character, emphasized for effect and, through the emphasis, peculiarly effective. It is never, in Dickens, simply that of the author; but in both the voice and the achievements of Inspector Bucket, the first police-detective in English fiction, there seem, without a doubt, to be some Dickensian traits.

Bucket is, of course, considerably more than a voice. He is a complex and formidable character; uncannily shrewd and intelligent; always courteous; compassionate, even to his prisoners; dedicated to his tasks; attractively idiosyncratic. But it is by the particular tones of his rhetoric that we remember Bucket most vividly. Two representative passages will show something of his linguistic range. Each uses repetitive rhetoric – one of Bucket's favourite devices – but for quite different purposes. In the first he prepares Sir Leicester for the shocking news he is about to give him of his wife:

'Now, Sir Leicester Dedlock, Baronet,' Mr Bucket begins, standing over him with one hand spread out on the library-table, and the forefinger of the other in impressive use, 'it's my duty to prepare you for a train of circumstances that may, and I go so far as to say that will, give you a shock. But, Sir Leicester Dedlock, Baronet, you are a gentleman; and I know what a gentleman is, and what a gentleman is capable of. A gentleman can bear a shock, when it must come, boldly and steadily. A gentleman can make up his mind to stand up against almost any blow. Why, take yourself, Sir Leicester Dedlock, Baronet. If there's a blow to be inflicted on you, you naturally think of your family. You ask yourself, how would all them ancestors of yours, away to Julius Caesar – not to go beyond him at present – have borne that blow? (ch. 54)

In the second, in the final scene at the Snagsbys, he shows up Mrs Snagsby's absurd suspicions of her husband, and at the same time illuminates the whole plot:

And Toughey – him as you call Jo – was mixed up in the same business, and no other; and the law-writer that you know of, was mixed up in the same business, and no other; and your husband, with no more knowledge of it than your great-grandfather, was mixed up (by Mr Tulkinghorn, deceased, his best customer) in the same business, and no other; and the whole bileing of the people was mixed up in the same business, and no other. And yet a married woman, possessing your attractions, shuts her eyes (and sparklers too), and goes and runs her delicate-formed head against a wall. Why, I am ashamed of you! (ch. 59)

A vital part of each passage is its flattery (if combined with exasperation in the second): a conscious flattery skilfully used as a weapon to persuade – but a very different kind in each passage, addressed unerringly to what matters most to each of his hearers. With Sir Leicester, his full, sonorous title (Bucket 'delights in a full title') begins the process; the appeal to him as a gentleman is its centre; the wonderfully absurd reference to 'all them ancestors of yours, away to Julius Caesar – not to go beyond him at present' is its natural sequel. With such language Sir Leicester can only be appeased. Mrs Snagsby is appeased too; but the flattery here is much cruder – playing on a purely physical vanity.

Bucket dominates much of the last part of the novel. He has his theatrical prop, the 'fat forefinger' that heralds 'a terrible avenger', as he moves inexorably towards Mlle Hortense's arrest. But it is the power wielded by his sheer intelligence that Dickens delights in showing. Much of this is an analytical power, as he puts together his case piece by piece; and Dickens skilfully extends it by showing its overt signs in Bucket's victim (signs that a host of later detective-stories were to imitate):

[Mlle Hortense's] step towards the door brings her front to front with Mr Bucket. Suddenly a spasm shoots across her face, and she turns deadly pale.

. . . 'What is the intention of this fool's play, say then?'
Mademoiselle demands, with her arms composedly crossed,
but with something in her dark cheek beating like a clock.

(ch. 54)

Bucket combines so many qualities, seems so super-
human in his solving of mysteries, is (as Dickens called
himself) so 'inimitable' in his language and tone of voice,
that it is surely possible to believe that, in some important
ways, Dickens saw much in common between the omniscient author and the omniscient detective:

Time and place cannot bind Mr Bucket. Like man in the
abstract, he is here to-day and gone to-morrow.   (ch. 53)

That conjures up the artist, untramelled by space and
time. 'But', adds Dickens to the description, 'very unlike
man indeed, he is here again the next day.' Bucket, with all
his ambiguities and hidden motives (never unsympathetic
in themselves to Dickens) is a highly practical, responsible
man too. Imagination coupled with responsibility was a
mixture Dickens valued, not only in others, but – with
justification – in himself.

Social groups

Novels 'of the social group' Edmund Wilson, in *Dickens:
The Two Scrooges* (1941), called Dickens's dense,
complex-plotted, later novels: *Bleak House, Little Dorrit,
Great Expectations, Our Mutual Friend*: 'the new *genre*'
that he said Dickens had invented. It is an excellent
description, so long as we recognize two things: that in
Bleak House especially, the 'group', the envisaged society
that contains the dense plots, is a parody-group, a parody
of the genuine organic society Dickens wanted intensely
to believe in; and that, as a parody-group, it is not
subservient to the laws of 'actuality'. In painting it,
Dickens could – and did – use all his imaginative gifts of

fantasy, exaggeration and theatrical effect. *Bleak House* is unsurpassed in its social range, from the highest in the land to the lowest: from the haughty baronet of ancient family, Sir Leicester Dedlock, to the destitute crossing-sweeper of literally no family at all, Jo. There were certainly county magnates of the Dedlock breed in England of the 1850s – just as there were many poor crossing-sweepers. But Sir Leicester's terror of another Peasants' Revolt, his conviction that one concession to the masses would open the floodgates and plunge the country into anarchy, adds more than a touch of theatre to him; it makes him – in the first half of the novel – that much more comically memorable. Again, Jo's death-scene has sufficient of the theatrical in it to make it for many readers (by no means all) one of the novel's authentic tragic moments.

What connects most of the disparate groups of *Bleak House* is the opposite of what *should* connect them: communal feeling, the sense of belonging to a society, or indeed positive feeling of any sort. It is, instead, rapacity, greed, muddle, disease and, above all – perhaps the main connecting-links of the novel – unreality, deadness, blindness, suspicion.

These are the intermeshing qualities of the world in which Dickens sets the mystery and violence of his main plot; with such a backcloth, the main plot becomes something far more complex and far more haunting than melodrama. In creating such a world, Dickens uses, as I have said, all his imaginative gifts. Its denizens are near enough human – or inhuman – types to be immediately recognizable. But the force they exert is much more than 'actual': it is nearer the demonic, the grotesque, the fantastic, or the totally unreal.

The major 'group' is, of course, the Court of Chancery, its parasites and its victims. The Lord Chancellor himself is a shadowy figure; it is his 'surrogate', 'Chancellor' Krook (one of the novel's many revealing names), owner of the Rag and Bottle Warehouse off Chancery Lane, who symbolizes the Court's evil force. But it is a grotesque force as well as an evil one. Krook is a devil, but a blackly comic one. Dickens's enjoyment in creating him – the sheer linguistic life and wit of his description – is everywhere apparent:

He was short, cadaverous, and withered; with his head sunk sideways between his shoulders, and the breath issuing in visible smoke from his mouth, as if he were on fire within.   (ch. 5)

Once we have the diabolic framework, the other details fit in. He is, naturally, drunken and illiterate. The grotesque muddle of his shop, with everything topsy-turvy and awry, is primarily a picture of Chancery; but pictures of a medieval Hell impinge too. 'One had only to fancy . . . that yonder bones in a corner, piled together and picked very clean, were the bones of clients' goes rather further than even Chancery's rapacity. As does Krook's 'familiar', the savage grey cat, Lady Jane, who at her master's bidding rips at a bundle of rags 'with her tigerish claws, with a sound that it set my teeth on edge to hear'. '"She'd do as much for any one I was to set her on"', said the old man.' His sudden touching of Ada's hair ('I have got three sacks of ladies' hair below, but none so beautiful and fine as this') adds the sensual detail that makes him Bluebeard as well as devil.

The tone in which Krook avows his reflection of Chancery is absurdly complacent, even proud; it adds the right half-comic dimension to the picture:

'I have a liking for rust and must and cobwebs . . . And I can't abear to part with anything I once lay hold of . . . That's the way I've got the ill name of Chancery. *I* don't mind. I go to see my noble and learned brother pretty well every day, when he sits in the Inn. He don't notice me, but I notice him. There's no great odds betwixt us. We both grub on in a muddle. (ch. 5)

But Krook's incessant watchfulness of John Jarndyce, his observation of him 'with the slyness of an old white fox', his 'curious expression of a sense of power', as he regards Jarndyce 'with eyes turned up and grey eyebrows lowered, until his eyes appeared to be shut' (ch. 14) are anything *but* comic. Here Dickens brings us very close to Chancery's truly sinister power; and the physical details and implications of the language anticipate both Kafka's *The Trial* and Orwell's *Nineteen Eighty-Four*.

This is the realm of the vampire; and twice we have that image in the novel. In ch. 11 Krook's lean hands, spread out above the just dead Nemo's body, are 'like a vampire's wings'; and, much later, when Richard is totally under the power of his attorney, Vholes, it is with a vampire, again, that Vholes is compared:

So slow, so eager, so bloodless and gaunt, I felt as if Richard were wasting away beneath the eyes of this adviser, and there were something of the Vampire in him.   (ch. 60)

Both of the major Chancery solicitors in the novel are presented as strikingly inhuman; but it is a mark of Dickens's new skills that their inhumanity is presented so differently. Tulkinghorn, as has been said earlier, is essentially reductive: all he touches he reduces to things; feelings, both others' and his own, have no existence for him. Hence his extraordinary power. Vholes (the vermin-name is significant, again) has reduced *himself*, deliberately drained the life out of himself, so as to appear, as he lies in waiting, to be no challenge to anyone. His language – and particularly the clichés he uses – sharply suggests this death-in-life: '"This", Vholes gives the desk one hollow blow again, "is your rock; it pretends to be nothing more."' '"Always here, sir. Personally, or by letter, you will always find me here, sir, with my shoulder to the wheel"' (ch. 39).

Everything about Vholes, in fact – his appearance, his

voice, his office in Symond's Inn – suggests death: death in himself and death for the client on whom he preys. Dickens makes little or no distinction between his black clothes and the man himself: Vholes 'takes off his close black gloves as if he were skinning his hands, lifts off his tight hat as if he were scalping himself' (ch. 29). At times he seems to be only his clothes: his 'dead glove . . . scarcely seemed to have any hand in it', says Esther; and she adds an image of haunting power: 'I thought of [his long thin shadow] on the outside of the coach, passing over all the sunny landscape between us and London, chilling the seed in the ground as it glided along' (ch. 45). His voice, 'half-audible', suggests 'an unclean spirit in him that will neither come out nor speak out'. His chambers, dirty, cramped, blinking 'at a dead wall', are (as houses and rooms always are in Dickens) an extension of himself. All the while he addresses Richard, his 'official cat watches [a] mouse's hole'. At his first appearance, when he arrives in Chesney Wold to summon Richard back to a hearing of Jarndyce and Jarndyce, 'the gaunt pale horse' that waits for them is clearly the emblem of Death from Revelations (one of many Biblical allusions in the novel); the reference to the Burial Service as he raps his hollow office desk, 'with a sound as if ashes were falling on ashes, and dust on dust', is even clearer.

Vholes has his touches of comedy too: his obsession with 'respectability' and his reiterated care for his aged father in the Vale of Taunton and his 'three raw-visaged, lank' daughters who live with him in a damp cottage in Kennington. But it is a grim comedy: 'respectability' is only the front behind which he preys on his clients; and his care for his daughters is seen as animal, not human: 'So might an industrious fox, or bear, make up his account of chickens or stray travellers with an eye to his cubs.' With such an adviser and predator, Richard has little chance;

Vholes's last appearance, as Jarndyce and Jarndyce comes to its predestined end, is appropriately as a gorged serpent (an image already used of his bags of documents): 'he gave one gasp as if he had swallowed the last morsel of his client, and his black buttoned-up unwholesome figure glided away to the door at the end of the Hall' (ch. 66).

If Vholes is imaged as a reptile, the Smallweeds, money-lending parasites of the Chancery world, are as near venomous insects and animals as human beings can be. Grandfather Smallweed's father was 'a horny-skinned, two-legged, money-getting species of spider'; the whole family 'bear a likeness to old monkeys with something on their minds'. They live underground, in what is more of a lair than a home. Dickens creates them as a grotesque and deadly parody of a family. They have no children, in the normal sense of the word: 'Little old men and women there have been, but no child' – except for Mrs Smallweed, who has reverted to infancy. They do not communicate. Mrs Smallweed screeches cadenzas on money – the only reality to either of them – 'like a horrible old parrot without any plumage'. Grandfather Smallweed hurls constant abuse at her, alternating with throwing a cushion at her head. Their whole sub-life is one of absolute reduction. Words are reduced to meaningless and repetitive vituperation: 'You are an old pig. You are a brimstone pig. You're a head of swine!' Smallweed himself, after such linguistic forays or the exertion of throwing the cushion, is reduced to a thing, a broken puppet.

But, like a nest of stinging insects, they are given a disturbing, unexpected power. Dickens handles the timing of their sudden appearances brilliantly. Tulkinghorn moves between town and country almost invisibly; Vholes glides on his visits to Richard like a serpent. The Smallweeds *irrupt* – on each occasion, of course, in the hope of gain: first, into Trooper George's shooting-gallery, in pursuit of hand-writing that will identify 'Nemo' as Lady Dedlock's former lover, Captain Hawdon; then, after a short spell in the Sols Arms, into Krook's shop, immediately after his death, 'to look after the property, as his heirs'; most grotesquely, into Sir Leicester's library, in the hope of blackmail; and, finally, into John Jarndyce's London lodgings, in the hope of selling him the new Jarndyce Will discovered at Krook's.

But each of these sudden appearances is more than plot-involvement. It is the irruption, each time, of a violent, corrupt, sub-natural world no less menacing for its grotesque comedy, or indeed for the unctuousness of Grandfather Smallweed's public front. The irruption of the *real* Smallweed, when he has Trooper George and Matthew Bagnet in his power over the bill that George cannot honour, comes in ch. 24 ('A Turn of the Screw') and has a disturbing realism to it:

'That's what [the letter] means, my dear friend. I'll smash you. I'll crumble you. I'll powder you. Go to the devil!'

The Smallweeds' taking over of Krook's shop (Mrs Smallweed turns out to be Krook's sister) is a particularly good example of what Dickens makes of an apparently arbitrary connexion. For Grandfather Smallweed becomes Krook's true heir: heir not only to 'the – the property! The property! – property!' (as he proclaims it to all and sundry), but to Krook's diabolism too. The vignette of the whole Smallweed family sorting endlessly through scraps of paper, consigned to the deep pit below the shop, continues the image of a medieval Hell.

What is remarkable is that Dickens makes the Smallweeds represent a clear philosophy at work: one that he consistently derided and exposed. To combine fantasy and conceptual realism in this way (as he does more daringly, and triumphantly, in Krook's Spontaneous Combustion) is integral to the art of *Bleak House*. In their 'practical character' ('always early to go out and late to marry'), the Smallweeds take the outlook of the calculating, statistical Mr Filer of *The Chimes* (1844) a stage further and anticipate, however crudely, Mr Gradgrind and his obsession with fact and hatred of fancy of Dickens's next novel, *Hard Times* (1854). They have 'discarded all amusements, discountenanced all story-books, fairy tales, fictions, and fables, and banished all levities whatsoever' (ch. 21). 'Judy never owned a doll, never heard of Cinderella, never played at any game.' And her twin-brother 'knows no more of Jack the Giant Killer, or of Sinbad the Sailor, than he knows of the people in the stars'. The Smallweed philosophy is made crystal-clear in an early exchange between grandfather and grandson:

'Been along with your friend again, Bart?'
  Small nods.
  'Dining at his expense, Bart?'
  Small nods again.
  'That's right. Live at his expense as much as you can, and take warning by his foolish example. That's the use of such a friend. The only use you can put him to', says the venerable sage.   (ch. 21)

It is precisely the calculating, exploitative philosophy practised by Gradgrind's star pupil, Bitzer.

The striking difference in treatment of the three Chancery victims points again to Dickens's new skills. The central victim is, of course, Richard Carstone; and the moving psychological study of his deterioration, presented both internally and externally, will be discussed later. Both the half-crazed little Miss Flite and the ruined and maddened Gridley, 'the man from Shropshire', are essentially comments on Richard's inevitable fate. But they are presented quite differently. Gridley is a voice, of terrible anger and terrible despair, inveighing against injustice; his explanation to John Jarndyce of what he has suffered, in ch. 15, is one of the grimmest and most indignant passages in the novel. He is the individual against the system, and quite helpless. '"There again!" said Mr Gridley, with no diminution of his rage. "The system! I am told, on all hands, it's the system."' The angry repetition here *is* the Gridley voice; and the more authentic, since it is Esther who records it and not the more expectedly indignant third-person narrator. We rarely see, or hear Gridley again, before his death-scene, but we do not need to. The butt of the lawyers in Court, imprisoned for contempt, hounded by Tulkinghorn, Gridley is a constant presence.

It is Esther again who reports Gridley's death; and the presence of Miss Flite with him in his last moments stresses the force created by pattern: here, the pattern of the final coming-together of the two Chancery victims, watched by Richard, the third:

Touchingly and awfully drawn together, he and the little mad woman were side by side, and, as it were, alone. She sat on a chair holding his hand, and none of us went close to them.

(ch. 24)

There is a Shakespearean power about this scene: perhaps a memory of the mad Lear and the blind Gloucester sitting reviling the world, by the shore at Dover.

Little Miss Flite is a strange mixture of fantasy and realism. Like Gridley, she is an omen; but both more delicate and, in her half-crazed state, more sinister:

'Oh!' said she. 'The wards in Jarndyce! Ve-ry happy, I am sure, to have the honour! It is a good omen for youth, and hope, and beauty, when they find themselves in this place, and don't know what's to come of it.'

(ch. 3)

A seemingly crazed fantasy prevails in this opening scene, as she awaits her judgment 'on the Day of Judgment' and

tells the wards of her discovery that the sixth seal of
Revelations is 'the Great Seal'. But almost every word
counts for the future too. Just as do the names of her
caged birds, when Krook reels them off in ch. 14. At the
end of the novel she releases them: not because she has her
judgment at last, as she had promised at the beginning;
but because the costs of Jarndyce and Jarndyce have
swallowed up its entire estate and Richard is dead from
the shock.

Formally, then, little Miss Flite, with her fantasies,
frames the novel: she is the embodiment, outside the
narrative, of what Chancery *does* to people in terms of
suffering and insanity. But Dickens makes her a real
person too, with a rôle to play in the plot and genuine
human relationships. She is important to Esther, prized
by Caddy, taken seriously as his patient by Allan
Woodcourt. It is Miss Flite who gives Esther the vital
news that Lady Dedlock had taken away the handker-
chief Esther had given to Jenny, the brickmaker's wife. It
is she again who helps Allan Woodcourt find a lodging for
the dying Jo in Trooper George's shooting-gallery. And
the warnings she gives Esther about the path Richard is
taking are at times far from fantastic:

'I know the signs, my dear. I saw them begin in Gridley. And I
saw them end. Fitz-Jarndyce, my love', speaking low again, 'I
saw them beginning in our friend the Ward in Jarndyce. Let
some one hold him back. Or he'll be drawn to ruin.' (ch. 35)

In her mixture of fantasy and realism, Miss Flite fulfils
an important part of the aim Dickens set himself in the
Preface: the dwelling 'upon the romantic side of familiar
things'.

The Chancery 'group' of *Bleak House* reveals to the full
rapacity, greed and muddle; just as its victims reveal
suffering and madness. Disease is just as strong a
connecting-link. Embodied in poor Jo, the crossing-

sweeper, the part it plays in bringing together the highest and the lowest 'groups' is a major theme of the novel. It is Jo's small-pox that afflicts Charley and disfigures Esther, before killing Jo himself. Though never stated, it is strongly suggested that the same contamination is the cause of Lady Dedlock's death too. Tom-All-Alone's, the London slum with its suggestive name that conjures up both isolation and alienation, is the physical centre of the disease at the heart of *Bleak House*. Disease-ridden itself, it spreads disease far and wide. Dickens makes it the title of a chapter (ch. 16): a chapter that begins with Sir Leicester sick of the gout in Chesney Wold and Lady Dedlock sick of boredom in the London house, and ends with Jo taking the disguised Lady Dedlock to her former lover's lodging, to the place of his inquest, and finally to the paupers' graveyard where he lies buried. The centre of the chapter is devoted to the horrors of Tom-All-Alone's and to a description of Jo's crossing-sweeping day. Thus, formally, we are confronted by the links between high and low. And Dickens never allows us to forget them. They point to the ineluctable theme of *Bleak House*: that, in the final count, we are all responsible for all.

We return to Tom-All-Alone's many more times; and two descriptions of it are particularly haunting. Linguistically, they work in quite different ways. In the first of them, the visit by Bucket and Snagsby in ch. 22, to look for Jo, the slum becomes momentarily an image of hell. Bucket and Snagsby are met by the corpse of a fever-victim; the crowd hovers round them, 'like a dream of horrible faces, and fades away up alleys and into ruins, and behind walls; and with occasional cries and shrill whistles of warning, thenceforth flits about them until they leave the place'.

The second description, which begins ch. 46, works through images too; but they are cosmic, not human, and they proceed by accumulation and analogy:

Darkness rests upon Tom-All-Alone's. Dilating and dilating since the sun went down last night, it has gradually swelled until it fills every void in the place . . . The moon has eyed Tom with a dull cold stare, as admitting some puny emulation of herself in his desert region unfit for life and blasted by volcanic fires; but she has passed on, and is gone. The blackest nightmare in his infernal stable grazes on Tom-All-Alone's, and Tom is fast asleep.

The wit and fancy there would normally invest its subject with animated life; here, it does the opposite; and we are left with a picture of darkness, desert and nightmare.

The figure of Jo himself, the only regular denizen of Tom-All-Alone's we are shown, blends, like little Miss Flite, fantasy and realism; though of a very different order to her's. He is at the same time a symbol of utter destitution and the real thing, a London street-urchin, observed with all Dickens's cold fury at the society that has bred him. Many of the vignettes of him are clearly symbolic: his sitting down to breakfast on the door-step of the Society for the Propagation of the Gospel in Foreign Parts and wondering 'what it's all about' (a clergyman wrote to Dickens in protest at this); his sitting under Blackfriars Bridge and gazing up at the golden cross above St Paul's, similarly mystified; and – the grimmest of the vignettes – his listening to street music with the drover's dog: 'probably with much the same amount of animal satisfaction . . . But, otherwise, how far above the human listener is the brute!' (ch. 16).

Jo is given too a substantial and realistic part to play in the plot; although, in his case, whether guiding the disguised Lady Dedlock to her lover's grave or playing his part in Bucket's trick to identify her, he is quite unconscious of what he is doing.

Jo's unconsciousness is part of his general ignorance: he can hardly be blamed for it. But Dickens makes unconsciousness of a very different kind a major link between other groups of characters in the novel; and this is presented as a serious moral flaw: a wilful attempt to evade reality, to escape the human condition. It links together characters totally disparate; what seems at first arbitrary comedy (for all play comic rôles of varying kinds) is seen to have beneath its surface a strong critical force. As a method of inquisition, such a device reminds us of Shakespeare's use of comedy in both the 'problem-plays' and tragedies. It points strongly to Dickens's new maturity.

These characters also blend fantasy and realism; but there is little of innocence in the mixture, as there is in little Miss Flite and in Jo. Skimpole, Mr Turveydrop and Chadband have already been discussed as 'voices': the most memorable in the novel. They are all parasites; and the fantasy-life of their language – entertaining as it is – is there chiefly as protective colouring. But as it grows (and each of them is gifted with a kind of spontaneous creativeness), the fantasy *replaces* reality. We are left with words over a void.

Presented as even more unreal are the aristocratic hangers-on at Chesney Wold, the multitude of poor Dedlock cousins, kept alive by Dedlock hospitality. These are the Dandies in religion and politics, and the elegant ladies and gentlemen 'who have agreed to put a smooth glaze on the world, and to keep down all its realities. For whom everything must be languid and pretty. Who have found out the perpetual stoppage' (ch. 12). As phantoms they flutter round Chesney Wold, attracted like moths by its light and warmth, with no life of their own. There is the 'debilitated cousin', the apogée of boredom, with a language to go with it; above all, there is Volumnia, compared to 'the little glass chandeliers of another age . . . with their meagre stems, their spare little drops . . . and their little feeble prismatic twinkling' (ch.

67), as she dances one night a year; and all of them are summed up in a particularly telling image (was Dickens remembering Satan's legions, 'Thick as autumnal leaves . . . In Vallombrosa', in *Paradise Lost*, bk I?), as they depart:

the one wintry wind that blows today shakes a shower from the trees near the deserted house, as if all the cousins had been changed into leaves. (ch. 28)

Two of the novel's best-known characters, the 'charitable' ladies, Mrs Jellyby and Mrs Pardiggle, have both long since ceased to engage with reality; but they evade different things and in different ways. Dickens beautifully contrasts them. Mrs Jellyby, plump and diminutive, has a serene look and handsome eyes; but they 'had a curious habit of seeming to look a long way off'. Her 'telepathic benevolence' allows her to see nothing immediately about her: her neglected and dirty children for ever tumbling down the stairs, the nightmare of her slovenly home, her silent husband with his head perpetually turned to the wall. All these Dickens turns into comical performances. Her plans for 'cultivating coffee and educating the natives of Borrioboola-Gha, on the left bank of the Niger' (ch. 4) have obliterated husband, children and home. Such lunatic idealism, however irresponsible, has a kind of comic pathos.

There is nothing pathetic at all about Mrs Pardiggle. Everything about her proclaims her insensitivity, both in body and soul. A 'formidable style of lady, with spectacles' and 'a prominent nose', she has a loud voice which impressed Esther's fancy 'as if it had a sort of spectacles on too'. She has only to come into a room to knock down objects with her skirts. A series of witty but ruthless images exposes her 'benevolence' as truly 'rapacious': in her field of action, the brickmaker's hovel, she pulls out a good book, 'as if it were a constable's staff', says Esther, and takes 'the whole family into custody. I mean into religious custody, of course; but she really did it as if she were an inexorable moral Policeman carrying them all off to a Station-house' (ch. 8). As one of the breakfast-party after Caddy's wedding, she further propagates her mission of 'pouncing upon the poor, and applying benevolence to them like a strait-jacket'. These images suggest performances too; but too near the bone to be comic. Dickens hated the wrong kind of 'charity' – interference masquerading as charity – even more than he disliked the wrong kind of idealism. Mrs Jellyby evades domestic reality and others have to bear the consequences. Mrs Pardiggle tramples on human respect and human privacy, all in the name of charity.

But having carefully drawn his portraits of the two ladies – and their exaggerations – separately, Dickens brings them together in his later ferocious picture of the dying Jo:

He is not one of Mrs Pardiggle's Tockahoopo Indians; he is not one of Mrs Jellyby's lambs; being wholly unconnected with Borrioboola-Gha; he is not softened by distance and unfamiliarity; he is not a genuine foreign-grown savage; he is the ordinary home-made article. Dirty, ugly, disagreeable to all the senses, in body a common creature of the common streets, only in soul a heathen.   (ch. 47)

To link the destitute Jo with the two ladies whose charity is not for him – just as he has been linked already with Lady Dedlock, with Tulkinghorn, with Skimpole – shows something of the remarkable structuring that has gone into the novel: something of Dickens's skill in creating an interconnected world out of materials so otherwise disparate.

Deliberately contrasted with those 'groups' in the novel who epitomize muddle or greed or blindness are the characters who, however comic or vulnerable or materially unsuccessful, keep a firm hold on reality: the Bagnets; Boythorn, in his own eccentric way; the Rouncewells; and even, in one important, if surprising, scene, the Bayham Badgers. The comedy that plays around them is not the new, inquisitorial comedy of much of the novel; it is much nearer the playful, affectionate, protective comedy of the early Dickens. Innocence is its primary quality; and, in the world of *Bleak House*, innocence needs considerable protection.

Even the generous and humane John Jarndyce is not immune from the all-pervading evasion of reality. In his case, retreat to 'the Growlery' and the fiction of the East wind are more comic than serious; but Dickens leaves us in no doubt of his blindness to the true Skimpole and to the charitable institutions only interested in him for his money.

The most obviously innocent characters in the novel are the Bagnets: Matthew, ex-artilleryman, now bassoon-player, Mrs Bagnet, and their three barrack-named children, Woolwich, Quebec and Malta; one of Dickens's few happy, united and attractive families. As seen by the sophisticated third-person narrator, they live in a comic framework of constantly repeated words and actions. The repetition here can be trying; but, ultimately, it is a strength, a guarantee of dependability. 'George', says Mr Bagnet to the trooper, who has asked his advice, 'You know me. It's my old girl that advises. She has the head. But I never own to it before her. Discipline must be maintained' (ch. 27). He says it many times; and each time we are more aware of the solidity of their relationship than of the absurdity of the fiction about discipline. Mrs Bagnet's repetition is of busy action: for ever 'washing greens' or serving the meals to her family on an 'exact system'. And, again, the effect is of trust: the ordinary, however humdrum or comically repeated, can be relied upon. When Mrs Bagnet is given her important part to play in the plot and trudges off to Lincolnshire to bring back Mrs Rouncewell to her imprisoned son in triumph, she goes off – as she had once made her 'way home to Europe' – with only her old grey cloak and umbrella and a few shillings in her purse. In all the frenetic unreality of much of *Bleak House*, the Bagnets are an oasis of warmth and reality; and the use of sympathetic repetition plays a considerable part in persuading us of their strength.

Repetition plays its part too in the exhilaratingly comic figure of Boythorn (modelled on Dickens's much-loved and eccentric friend Walter Savage Landor): here, a repetition of his extreme responses of boisterous laughter, ferocity and gentleness (his little canary perched on his shoulder as he inveighs against Sir Leicester or a coach-man). But Boythorn is much more than a comically endearing figure. His exaggerations may be quite ir-rational; as is his vehement dispute over the right-of-way with Sir Leicester. But his fundamental goodness is clear and Jarndyce points unerringly to his inner worth: 'the inside of the man, the warm heart of the man, the passion of the man, the fresh blood of the man'. The scene in ch. 18 in which Boythorn opposes principle to Skimpole's total lack of it, in both paying homage to Sir Leicester and objecting to him (since Boythorn does), may be treated half-comically, but it goes to the heart of the contrast in values at the centre of the novel.

The dialogue in which it is done is formal, not naturalistic. Dickens moves Skimpole, as in a game of chess, from social respect for Sir Leicester to total acceptance of the social system; just as he moves Boythorn from refusal to accept Sir Leicester to the existence or not of principle. But it works with total success. Dickens is a novelist, not a philosopher. He can leave out the logical moves, the gradations of abstract argument, precisely because he has already established in other ways what matters to him – and to us – about his speakers. He has already made Boythorn's garden, at the old Parsonage house, a symbol in its maturity, abundance and orderliness, of Boythorn's sense of principle.

The Rouncewells are given their important and solid place in the novel much more naturalistically. Physical details play a considerable part. Mrs Rouncewell, the old housekeeper at Chesney Wold, is 'handsome, stately, wonderfully neat'; her stays, that might have been a 'broad old-fashioned family fire-grate', perfectly express her reliability, her devotion to the Dedlock family and to Chesney Wold itself. Trooper George, her younger son, the 'vagabond' – as he calls himself – is every inch an ex-Dragoon, his massive presence stressed by contrasts. He is a giant to the stunted Grandfather Smallweed's pigmy, 'a broadsword to an oyster-knife'. His shooting-gallery near Leicester Square, functional, unadorned, with its mattresses on the floor and its cold water-pump, reflects, as we would expect, his simple integrity. The devotion of his eccentric handyman, the smoky and battered little Phil Squod – one of Dickens's memorable and at times touching grotesques – reflects it too; just as does George's own sympathy with Phil. The Rouncewell world – like the Bagnet world – is one in which human affections, beneath the bluff exteriors, are delicately and imaginatively shown. The contrast with the world of Chancery could not be sharper.

The details that give us most of what we know of George's elder brother, the ironmaster, are not of himself, but of his work. And his work, as a progressive industrialist, is clearly what fired Dickens's imagination. As a boy, Rouncewell constructed 'steam-engines out of saucepans'; as a successful ironmaster, he attracts one of

Dickens's very rare, detailed, yet fanciful descriptions of industrial activity.

The picture of the iron lying about in his factory in the North, 'in every stage, and in a vast variety of shapes', stresses the creativity of this kind of work, its state of perpetual change:

> distant furnaces of it glowing and bubbling in its youth; bright fireworks of it showering about, under the blows of the steam-hammer; red-hot iron, white-hot iron, cold-black iron; and iron taste, an iron smell, and a Babel of iron sounds.   (ch. 62)

Dickens may have been ambivalent in his attitude to 'progress'; but we cannot miss the excitement in that description ('distant furnaces of it glowing and bubbling in its youth; bright fireworks of it showering about, under the blows of the steam-hammer'). The ironmaster symbolizes something new; but it is a *real* world as well as a new one, and the value of its reality is made clear in one of the great comic set-scenes of the novel: the scene in the Chesney Wold drawing-room in which Rouncewell requests that his son's *fiancée* should leave her service in Chesney Wold to complete her education. Again, as with Boythorn and Skimpole earlier, Dickens needs little in the way of argument. What matters can be done tellingly as comic performance. On the one side we have Sir Leicester, the epitome of the past, convinced that any concession will bring another Peasants' Revolt, led by another Wat Tyler (and Dickens could not resist naming Rouncewell's son Watt); on the other side, the ironmaster, son of Sir Leicester's housekeeper, the new and successful industrialist. Reference by Rouncewell to a factory-owner's son brings the crisis:

> Sir Leicester's magnificence explodes. Calmly, but terribly.
>
> 'Mr Rouncewell', says Sir Leicester, with his right hand in the breast of his blue coat – the attitude of state in which he is painted in the gallery: 'do you draw a parallel between Ches-

ney Wold, and a –' here he resists a disposition to choke – 'a
factory?'   (ch.28)

What all three Rouncewells stand for – the mark of
their reality among all the shifting unreality offered by the
world of *Bleak House* – is faithful service; even if, for two
of them, it is service to the past. For Mrs Rouncewell,
service to Chesney Wold is her life; even when 'the great
old Dedlock family' breaks up and 'passion and pride . . .
have died away' from the house, she will continue to serve
what is left. For Trooper George, who has done his
service as a soldier, it is the decision to be 'officered' again,
to return to help Sir Leicester, rather than to join his
brother in his business. For the ironmaster it is service to
the new: to the material, iron-born creativity of his 'great
undertakings'.

At first sight, the Bayham Badgers, the last of these
'groups', seem to be pure comic relief, there for their joint
obsession with Mrs Badger's two former husbands,
'Captain Swosser of the Royal Navy' and 'Professor
Dingo of European reputation'. On the Badgers' second
appearance, though, when they show their anxieties
about Richard's medical studies, Mrs Badger – echoed by
her husband – is given a more serious function. Her
language is still comic, but the point she makes in both
reminiscences is as relevant to the novel's contrast of
values as is the 'argument' on principle between Boythorn
and Skimpole in the chapter that follows it:

'It was a maxim of Captain Swosser's,' said Mrs Badger,
'speaking in his figurative naval manner, that when you make
pitch hot, you cannot make it too hot; and that if you only have
to swab a plank, you should swab it as if Davy Jones were after
you.

'People objected to Professor Dingo, when we were staying in
the North of Devon, after our marriage', said Mrs Badger, 'that
he disfigured some of the houses and other buildings, by

chipping off fragments of the edifice with his little geological hammer. But the Professor replied, that he knew of no building, save the Temple of Science.   (ch. 17)

Both the nautical language and the wit here are enjoyable in themselves; they also give the stamp of truth to what is being said. 'When you make pitch hot, you cannot make it too hot' has implications far beyond naval discipline; the jump of wit from material buildings to 'the Temple of Science' points to what should be the dedication of every vocation. Dickens can make comedy do a great many serious things.

Irony

Irony is the most dominant tone of the third-person narrator: a dark irony that, reflecting omniscience, pretends to objectivity, but is quickly seen to mask a whole range of tones, from sarcastic derision to indignation and anger. Derision is most obvious in the accounts of fashionable society, of life at Chesney Wold: of Sir Leicester in his magisterial complacency, of Lady Dedlock in her elegant boredom, of the Dandies in politics and religion. The world of Chancery is too powerful and destructive to be simply derided; there is, of course, considerable sarcasm in the picture of fog and stagnation that mirrors the Court in the opening chapter; but, as Krook's shop, in its appalling muddle and greed, becomes the new mirror and as, in turn, we see Tulkinghorn and Vholes at work, the dominant, if still hidden, tone is clearly indignation. Real anger, still masked as objectivity, is reserved for the portrait of Jo. We can see the power of Dickens's irony in two of Jo's set-scenes: his 'evidence' at Nemo's inquest and the scene with the disguised Lady Dedlock at her lover's grave.

The irony of Jo's answers at the inquest is given its full

ferocity by their context. The end of the previous chapter (ch. 11) and the beginning of this ('Our Dear Brother') have given us the horror of the law-writer's death. But, from then on, most of the scene is comic, dominated by the absurd beadle, the boys who taunt him, and Little Swills, the comic vocalist. The inquest itself is treated in the same vein. It is in this setting that Dickens gives us, in Jo's answers, his picture of absolute ignorance. The savage parody of the Catechism enhances its effect:

Name, Jo. Nothing else that he knows on. Don't know that everybody has two names. Never heerd of sich a think. Don't know that Jo is short for a longer name. Thinks it long enough for *him*. *He* don't find no fault with it. Spell it? No. *He* can't spell it. No father, no mother, no friends. Never been to school. What's home? Knows a broom's a broom, and knows it's wicked to tell a lie. Don't recollect who told him about the broom, or about the lie, but knows both. Can't exactly say what'll be done to him arter he's dead if he tells a lie to the gentlemen here, but believes it'll be something wery bad to punish him, and serve him right – and so he'll tell the truth.

(ch. 11)

This is England in 1852; and, as we know (see p. 8), modelled on a real boy's evidence two years earlier. The response, by both Coroner and audience, adds total insensitivity to the picture; its comic thrust increases the irony:

'Don't you think you can receive his evidence, sir?' asks an attentive Juryman.
   'Out of the question', says the Coroner. 'You have heard the boy. "Can't exactly say" won't do, you know. We can't take *that*, in a Court of Justice, gentlemen. It's terrible depravity. Put the boy aside.'
   Boy put aside; to the great edification of the audience; – especially of Little Swills, the Comic Vocalist.

The major irony of the scene, a few chapters later, in which Jo shows Lady Dedlock her lover's graveyard, is the physical conjunction in one place of the highest and the lowest in the novel: a scene imprinted indelibly on our memory by Phiz's illustration, 'Consecrated Ground'. It is the formal answer to Dickens's own deliberate question, posed earlier in the same chapter (quoted already): 'What connexion can there be, between the place in Lincolnshire, the house in town . . . and the whereabouts of Jo the outlaw with the broom . . .?' Dickens, of course, knows the answer – as the reader, at that point, could not. It is a legitimate part of the author's omniscience. And the irony is increased by comedy, again: in this place of horror, a particularly gruesome comedy dependent on words and word-play:

'Is this place of abomination, consecrated ground?' [asks Lady Dedlock].
   'I don't know nothink of consequential ground', says Jo, still staring.
   'Is it blessed?'
   'WHICH?' says Jo, in the last degree amazed.
   'Is it blessed?'
   'I'm blest if I know', says Jo, staring more than ever; 'but I shouldn't think it warn't. Blest?' repeats Jo, something troubled in his mind. 'It an't done it much good if it is. Blest? I should think it was t'othered myself. But I don't know nothink!'
                                                                            (ch. 16)

The ironies of Jo's set-scenes are of tone. But the novel's major ironies are of plot too: most obviously in the main plot's revelation that Lady Dedlock and Esther are mother and daughter; but also in the carefully worked-out techniques Dickens uses to reveal, stage by stage, incident by incident, the very different fates of Tulkinghorn and Richard; and, finally, in the treatment of the afflicted Sir Leicester, as he waits for his fled wife's return. Each of these deserves detailed treatment.

Tulkinghorn's remorselessness in tracking down Lady Dedlock's past is a main thread of *Bleak House*. The

devices by which he does so occupy much of the first
three-quarters of the novel. The irony is that, as he puts
together, piece by piece, the facts that will irrevocably
lead to Lady Dedlock's exposure, so, unknown to him –
or to anyone else – Mlle Hortense is plotting his own
death. 'Closing in', the title of ch. 48, which ends with his
murder, anticipates 'Springing a Mine', the final revelation of Lady Dedlock's past, by six chapters;
Tulkinghorn never sees his victim's disgrace, however
ruthlessly he has brought it about. Dickens deliberately
places him on a curve leading first to success and
ultimately – just when that success is within his grasp – to
his murder.

The relationship between Tulkinghorn and Lady
Dedlock is drawn with great subtlety. They begin almost
evenly matched, each watchful and suspicious of the
other; as Tulkinghorn gains the ascendancy, his new
power shows itself in small, skilfully managed changes of
voice; his courtesy, now that he knows all, is a weapon:

'Sir', she returns, without looking up from the ground, on
which her eyes are now fixed, 'I had better have gone. It would
have been far better not to have detained me. I have no more to
say.'
'Excuse me, Lady Dedlock, if I add, a little more to hear.'
(ch. 41)

Dickens has been charged by some critics with exaggerat-
ing almost all his effects. He does so, deliberately and in
general enjoyably, when the situation requires it; but the
subtle, low-keyed change in Tulkinghorn's voice in that
exchange shows what a mastery Dickens has of the tonal
minutiae of such relationships as well.

It is in this chapter too that Dickens first strongly hints
that the Tulkinghorn curve will change; that Fate has
something new in store for him:

Away in the moonlight lie the woods and fields at rest, and the
wide house is as quiet as the narrow one. The narrow one!

Where are the digger and the spade, this peaceful night, destined to add the last great secret to the many secrets of the Tulkinghorn existence? Is the man born yet, is the spade wrought yet?

Dickens uses the same ironical technique in this passage as he will use before the murder itself seven chapters later: the setting of the pastoral scene before, here, the symbols of death; as, there, before the horror of the murder itself.

'Begin grim shadow on him' was Dickens's memorandum note for that chapter. In ch. 48, 'Closing in', the chapter that ends with Tulkinghorn's murder, the omens take over. They do it by what Dickens makes us feel is a deliberate, malevolent failure to warn him. The splendid clock upon the staircase, his own watch, the high chimney-stacks in the street – none of them will say, 'Don't go home!' Not even 'Allegory', the Roman pointing from the ceiling, will warn him, 'Don't come here!' But Dickens gives the omens a haunting power ('If it said now, Don't go home! *High and mighty street*' was his note for this chapter); and this makes the discovery of the murder itself much more than merely melodramatic.

The treatment of Lady Dedlock after Tulkinghorn's murder adds an appropriately ironical epilogue. We know how she has dreaded him, wished him dead. Now, falsely accused of the murder, she almost believes that she *has* committed it. Dickens shows marvellous penetration here into a guilt-ridden mind; and one phrase shows his imaginative insight as he makes her terror physical: 'she shudders as if the hangman's hands were at her neck'. But her real terror is that, even in death, Tulkinghorn is still pursuing her; and, in a series of remarkable passages, Dickens shows us just how obsession advances in such a mind. They culminate in a striking image: 'What was his death but the keystone of a gloomy arch removed, and now the arch begins to fall in a thousand fragments, each crushing and mangling piecemeal.' In 'The Macabre in

Dickens' (*All in Good Time*, 1955), Humphry House well described the overwhelming impression such passages give us: that Dickens is working 'as much beneath the surface as above it', communicating, in such a crisis as Lady Dedlock's, 'the ultimate loneliness of human life'.

There is no dramatic change in the curve of Richard Carstone's fate, as there is in Tulkinghorn's; once Chancery has exerted its sinister power over him, it is all downward. The irony arises out of contrasted states of knowledge, where the audience knows much more than the hero. Here, Dickens makes Jarndyce and Esther, as well as the reader, increasingly aware of the deterioration in Richard and the reason for it, while Richard himself goes blindly on. His own awareness at the beginning of Chancery's baleful influence and his conviction that it cannot touch *him* make the irony acute; as does the singularly attractive portrait we are given of him: 'as frank and generous a nature as there can possibly be', as Esther says. But Dickens's memoranda notes reveal his early plans for Richard's deterioration. 'New traits in Richard Yes – slightly' is the note for part 3 (chs. 8 and 9); 'Richard? YES. carry through his character – developing itself' is that for part 6 (chs. 17 and 18). Where Dickens breaks new ground is in this impressive study of a weak character 'developing itself'. We see how everything fits: his carelessness over money; his inability to settle into any profession; his twisting and turning in his attempts to persuade Esther of his own rightness in making Jarndyce and Jarndyce 'the object of [his] life'.

The most ironically painful of the many signs of Richard's decline is his estrangement from John Jarndyce, his benefactor. Dickens makes Jarndyce fully aware of the workings of Richard's mind:

'Dear, unfortunate, mistaken Richard', [says Esther]. 'When will he awake from his delusion?' 'he is not in the way to do so now, my dear', replied my guardian. 'The more he suffers, the more averse he will be to me: having made me the principal representative of the great occasion of his suffering.' (ch. 60)

The psychological rightness of this seemingly paradoxical attitude was clearly of the greatest interest to Dickens. He returns to it many times in the novel. And, to examine Richard from the inside, he evolves an analytical, 'internal' language, which we shall not find again, used with such assurance and understanding, until the analysis of Arthur Clennam in *Little Dorrit*:

But injustice breeds injustice; the fighting with shadows and being defeated by them, necessitates the setting up of substances to combat; from the impalpable suit which no man alive can understand, the time for that being long gone by, it has become a gloomy relief to turn to the palpable figure of the friend who would have saved him from this ruin, and make *him* his enemy . . . it is a justification to him in his own eyes to have an embodied antagonist and oppressor.   (ch. 39)

That is the view of the omniscient third-person narrator: it has the ring of truth. But Dickens insists on an outside view as well. From the beginning he makes little Miss Flite supply this: first, by treating her on every meeting as an omen for Richard's fate; then, with a telling irony, by virtually identifying him with her as Chancery victim. (It is Esther who identifies them; and we rarely doubt her judgment):

So young and handsome, and in all respects so perfectly the opposite of Miss Flite! And yet, in the clouded, eager, seeking look that passed over him, so dreadfully like her!   (ch. 37)

When Richard is on the edge of ruin, Miss Flite makes the identification closer still. 'My dear', she tells Esther, 'next to myself he is the most constant suitor in Court. He begins quite to amuse our little party.' And she confides to Esther her two secrets: she has made Richard her executor ('Nominated, constituted, and appointed him in my will. Ye-es.'); and she has added two more to her collection of birds: 'I call them the Wards in Jarndyce. They are caged up with all the others' (ch. 39).

It needs the collapse of the case of Jarndyce and Jarndyce to break Richard's spell. Dickens allows him the end of his delusion and shows him reconciled with John Jarndyce; but only on his death-bed. And little Miss Flite is appropriately given the last ironical word:

When all was still, at a late hour, poor crazed Miss Flite came weeping to me, and told me she had given her birds their liberty.
(ch. 65)

Two very distinct kinds of irony operate in 'A Wintry Day and Night', Dickens's treatment of the afflicted Sir Leicester. The reader knows that, after her letter and the torment that led to her writing it, Lady Dedlock will never return. There is an obvious irony in Sir Leicester's self-deceptions, as he tries desperately to persuade himself that she will: in his having her rooms at all times ready for her homecoming; in refusing to have the candles lit, so as to persuade himself it is still day. Again, as in the prelude to Tulkinghorn's murder, Dickens keeps repeating a refrain to underline the irony: 'Who will tell him?' But its tone is altogether different: this is an irony that directs our full sympathy to Sir Leicester's situation.

But the portrait of Sir Leicester contains another kind of irony, directed against the over-simplifying reader. For much of the novel Sir Leicester has been a caricature, almost a buffoon, a radical's picture of 'deadlockery'. In this chapter he is humane and dignified, oblivious of all wrong to himself, anxious only that all should know he is on unaltered terms with his wife. Dickens gives him an accolade allowed to few of his characters:

His noble earnestness, his fidelity, his gallant shielding of her, his generous conquest of his own wrong and his own pride for her sake, are simply honourable, manly, and true.   (ch. 58)

The change is not as arbitrary as it may seem. Gallantry to his wife was stressed on his first appearance; her name, pronounced 'in a tone of mourning and compassion rather than reproach', was on his lips as he sank to the ground after his stroke. But Dickens is making an important point about the complexity and paradoxes of human nature. The sympathy produced by the conjunction of both kinds of irony makes the chapter perhaps the most moving in the novel.

Set-scenes

Set-scenes, often, though by no means always, of violent action, play a powerful part in Dickens's novels; and *Bleak House* has more than most. They clearly satisfy a strong theatrical urge in Dickens; but, formally, they do much more. They act, as we should expect, as climaxes to particular parts of the narration; but, beyond that, they create feelings beyond the capacity of the narrative itself to do. As 'stops' in time, they exert a peculiar timeless force. It underlines the bleakness of *Bleak House* that almost all such set-scenes should be of death: violent, sinister, or darkly ironic. Tulkinghorn's murder has already been discussed as a key example of Dickens's ironical power. Four more deaths are the subject of set-scenes: the discovery of the dead Nemo; Krook's 'Spontaneous Combustion'; Jo's death; and the finding of the body of Lady Dedlock.

The two chapters (10 and 11) which describe Tulkinghorn's discovery of the dead law-writer Nemo in Krook's house, the inquest on him, and his burial, together perhaps form the most powerful succession of set-scenes in the novel. Several things contribute to this. Most unusually, the two chapters run on, with no break in the narrative; they also give us a brilliant example of

Dickens's use of suspense: ch. 10, describing Tulkinghorn's first sight of Nemo on his bed in his squalid
opium-filled room, ends part 3 of the novel; the original
readers had to wait a month for ch. 11 to realise that
Nemo was dead. But, tonally, what is most striking is the
mixture of horror and comedy throughout. It is as though
the one magnetically attracts the other. Ch. 10 begins with
the mainly comic treatment of the Snagsby establishment
and ends with the horror of Nemo's room. In ch. 11 the
conjunction is even closer. The Scottish doctor is almost
pure 'comic relief', as is Little Swills, the vocalist, when he
describes the inquest the same night to a comic refrain.
The inquest itself, largely comic (with the disturbing
exception of Jo's questioning), is followed by the savage
parody of the Burial Service: 'here, they lower our dear
brother down a foot or two: here, sow him in corruption,
to be raised in corruption'.

One particular image runs like a *leitmotif* through both
chapters: the 'two gaunt holes', pierced through the
drawn shutters of Nemo's room, seen as eyes staring in.
Three times they are referred to as an integral part of the
sinister surroundings. But the final time, towards the end
of ch. 11, there is a difference:

Then there is rest around the lonely figure now laid in its last
earthly habitation; and it is watched by the gaunt eyes in the
shutters through some quiet hours of night.

It would be too much to say that the 'eyes' are now
benign; but the new rhythm of the prose clearly enacts the
peace that is now its subject.

There is a new tone too – and a new attitude to Nemo –
in the final vignette which closes ch. 11: the picture of Jo
sweeping the step at the entrance to the graveyard. The
comment on it is Dickens's own, no longer the impersonal
narrator's:

Jo, is it thou? Well, well! Though a rejected witness, who 'can't exactly say' what will be done to him in greater hands than men's, thou art not quite in outer darkness. There is something like a distant ray of light in thy muttered reason for this:

'He was wery good to me, he was!'

What makes the set-scene – or the succession of set-scenes – in these two chapters so powerful is precisely this mixture of tones. In no novel before *Bleak House* has Dickens conveyed to us so strikingly the complexity and the multi-facetedness of experience.

Krook's 'Spontaneous Combustion' (ch. 32) is the most celebrated and melodramatic set-scene in the novel, if not in all Dickens's novels. The controversy it gave rise to at the time is discussed later (pp. 91–2). What makes it a compelling *coup de théâtre* is Dickens's highly skilful use of suspense: above all, the creation of dense and horrific detail to set the atmosphere. Everything in the chapter – the uneasy conversation between Snagsby and Jobling, the long and increasingly menacing wait in Jobling's room, the guttering candle 'with a great cabbage head and a long winding-sheet', the 'thick yellow liquor' that defiles Guppy's hand – contributes to the suspense. Krook's cat, snarling at 'the something on the ground', plays her part in the finale. But the device that finally and fully involves us in the horror is a linguistic one, a change in the point-of-view: as Guppy and Jobling find the small cinder, all that remains of Krook, 'they' become 'we'; we are *all* involved in the ghastly sight:

O Horror, he IS here! and this from which we run away, striking out the light and overtaking one another into the street, is all that represents him.

And it is *we* who cry for help:

Help, help, help! come into this house for Heaven's sake!

Dickens uses the same device to great dramatic effect, to involve us in the flight from Paris at the end of *A Tale of*

Two Cities. There too the protagonists, Jarvis Lorry, Lucie and her husband and father, as they escape the terrors of the Revolution, suddenly become 'us': 'The wind is rushing after us, and the clouds are flying after us, and the moon is plunging after us.'

But the metaphorical implications of Krook's death make it much more than a brilliant stroke of theatre. The chapter-title, 'The Appointed Time', gives it the status of Fate: it is the long-wished, irrevocable combustion of Chancery, of 'all authorities . . . where false pretences are made and where injustice is done'. And, to enforce his effect, Dickens changes narrative to apostrophe and directs his rhetoric to the highest in the land – and, of course, to the reader as well:

Call the death by any name Your Highness will, attribute it to whom you will, or say it might have been prevented how you will, it is the same death eternally – inborn, inbred, engendered in the corrupt humours of the vicious body itself, and that only – Spontaneous Combustion, and none other of all the deaths that can be died.

The death of Jo was regarded by many of Dickens's contemporaries as one of the most powerful scenes in all his writing. Others have found it too emotional; others, again, have objected to the use Dickens made in it of the Lord's Prayer. The pointing of the scene by the words of the best-known prayer in Christendom, of which Jo understands hardly a word, shows in fact the skill with which Dickens turns a universally known plea – the plea for supernatural help and compassion – into a savagely ironical comment. It is a comment directed mainly against the futility of formal religion to help Jo and his kind in their ignorance; underlined by the humanity of the watchers by Jo's bed, Woodcourt, who speaks the opening words of the prayer, Trooper George and Phil:

'Jo, can you say what I say?'
'I'll say anythink as you say, sir, fur I knows it's good.'

'Our Father.'
'Our Father! – yes, that's wery good, sir.'
'Which art in Heaven.'
'Art in Heaven – is the light a-comin, sir?'
'It is close at hand. Hallowed be thy name!'
'Hallowed be – thy –'

The light is come upon the dark benighted way. Dead! Dead, your Majesty. Dead, my lords and gentlemen. Dead, Right Reverends and Wrong Reverends of every order. Dead, men and women, born with Heavenly compassion in your hearts. And dying thus around us every day.　　　　　(ch. 47)

Two linguistic devices should be noted here. First, the change from description to apostrophe as Jo dies ('Dead, your Majesty. Dead, my lords and gentlemen') deliberately implicates every reader. Direct anger has taken over from irony, even if only momentarily. And, secondly, the final sentence ('And dying thus around us every day') has fallen into blank verse: it is a perfect pentameter. Such a poetic effect, whether conscious or unconscious (and Dickens had earlier claimed to a correspondent that such effects were unconscious), helps to give the whole scene a timeless power outside its place in the narrative-structure: Jo's death has become considerably more than the death of the character Jo.

One delicate touch, as Jo lies dying, could almost go unnoticed; it is the nearest Dickens comes to registering any of the onlookers' grief. Woodcourt signs to Phil to carry his table and hammer out of Jo's room. 'When the little hammer is next used, there will be a speck of rust upon it', says the narrator. Quite different as is the intent, we may well remember Othello: 'Put up your bright swords, or the dew will rust them.'

The dramatic pursuit that ends with the discovery of Lady Dedlock dead at the graveyard (chs. 57 and 59) is narrated entirely by Esther. The choice of point-of-view is significant. Dickens could have related the events in the guise of his third-person narrator; the focus could have been on Lady Dedlock herself or Sir Leicester or Bucket, or alternated between the three of them. By making Esther the narrator, Dickens is stressing her importance as heroine. He also impressively extends the range and quality of her experience. What she goes through externally is frightening enough: the frenzied carriage-drive night and day through snow and sleet; the unspoken belief, shared with Bucket, that her mother is bent on suicide and they may find her too late. No nineteenth-century novelist knew more than Dickens of the details of such a drive – of what both horses and passengers suffered from the appalling state of the roads and weather – or could communicate them so realistically. It is one of the dramatic triumphs of the novel. But Dickens's ambition goes much further. It is Esther's *internal* suffering, her moments of heightened consciousness, that he forces the reader to share; and he registers these, with remarkable precision, through the analogy of dreams or nightmares.

The first of such moments comes soon after they leave, when Bucket questions the Thames Police:

I remained quiet; but what I suffered in that dreadful spot I never can forget. And still it was like the horror of a dream. A man yet dark and muddy, in long swollen sodden boots and a hat like them, was called out of a boat, and whispered with Mr Bucket, who went away with him down some slippery steps – as if to look at something secret he had to show. They came back, wiping their hands upon their coats, after turning over something wet; but thank God it was not what I feared! (ch. 57)

Esther's terror here is precise: the terror that it is her mother's body the police have found. But it is conjured up by deliberately suggestive details: the 'long swollen sodden boots', which themselves suggest a body; the 'something secret' one of the men had to show; the 'something wet' they turned over. Esther's agony, as she watches helplessly, is that of the nightmare-victim rooted to the ground.

The Thames itself, always one of Dickens's most powerful symbols, gives birth to perhaps the most haunting image in the two chapters: Esther's transformation of the light of the carriage-lamps reflected by the river into 'a face, rising out of the dreadful water'. This, of course, is a trick played by the imagination: Lady Dedlock has not drowned herself. But Dickens displays great skill both in keeping the horrific possibility constantly before us and in showing its effects on Esther's consciousness.

The climax of this kind of writing – and Dickens had never sustained it for as long as he does in these two chapters – comes as they finally approach the burial-ground. Esther's memory is, at first, faithful to events: to the sharp impact of physical detail:

I recollect a few chilled people passing in the streets. I recollect the wet housetops, the clogged and bursting gutters and water-spouts, the mounds of blackened ice and snow over which we passed, the narrowness of the courts by which we went.

Then it changes; and she has the strange sensation of experiencing what she knows to be unreal as 'more substantial than the real' and at the same time of knowing that she does so. Dickens knows that the kind of consciousness he has created, stretched and heightened in Esther, cannot, in such a crisis, stand the full horror of reality. When the crisis comes, Esther *has* to deceive herself: 'I saw before me, lying on the step, the mother of the dead child. . . . She lay there, who had so lately spoken to my mother.' The reality, when there is no choice but to accept it, gives us the most truly dramatic moment in the novel:

I passed on to the gate, and stooped down. I lifted the heavy head, put the long dark hair aside, and turned the face. And it was my mother, cold and dead.

The set-scene that that completes – for the whole of the pursuit is, for Dickens, a set-scene – may be highly theatrical; it also shows what has not infrequently been denied: Dickens's unerring psychological insight. To have explored the mind of a girl, undergoing such an experience, with this delicacy and understanding, is further proof of Dickens's impressive advance as an artist in *Bleak House*.

It may seem unusual to treat the pastoral ending of the novel as a set-scene: it is neither dramatic nor 'numinous' nor psychologically exploratory. But Dickens himself attached great importance to his endings: no surviving character is left out (in *Dombey and Son* Florence's dog, Diogenes, had to be fitted in in proof); and the atmosphere – almost always, of peace after a storm – is created with great care. Dickens clearly does his best – not always with success – to give the pastoral ending feelings and implications beyond the mere completion in time of the narrative.

The vast canvas of characters in *Bleak House* necessitates an ending that extends to two chapters; and the structure of the two narrators is maintained to the end. Tonally, the chapters are very different. 'Down in Lincolnshire', the final account by the third-person narrator, is nostalgic and distanced. Its opening sets the tone: 'There is a hush upon Chesney Wold in these altered days, as there is upon a portion of the family history'; its close may be quoted again: 'passion and pride, even to the stranger's eye, have died away from the place in Lincolnshire, and yielded it to dull repose'. What is left of

the Chesney Wold group is here; Trooper George has
been re-absorbed; even the Bagnets are visitors. But the
language, bereft of passion and pride, has little sparkle;
what life it has comes in the satire of Volumnia; and,
without Sir Leicester's former grandeur or the absurdities
of the Dandies to fuel it, it has lost its old force.

'The Close of Esther's Narrative', the final chapter, is
very different: both from the third-person narrator's and
from her own previous chapters. There is a new time-
scale: she now speaks from the security of seven years on.
Dickens clearly intended to imbue the pastoral scene she
paints – happy marriage, children, Woodcourt's un-
worldly success, the 'new' Bleak House – with those
qualities that would make this a 'set-scene' of life, as
against all the scenes of death the novel has given us. But
he fails to do so. It is, again, a matter of language. In the
pursuit-chapters Dickens made us see Esther's experience
from the inside, at its strongest moments through the use
of dream-sequences; no comparable mechanism is employed here, or perhaps could be. The pastoral description Esther gives of the new Bleak House in ch. 64 – before
she knows it is her's – obviously underpins the final
chapter; but rustic images of sparkling water, trees and
flowers have hardly the substance of the appallingly grim
urban world so much of the novel has built up.

This new Bleak House, well away from London – and
indeed from the industry that Dickens generally as-
sociates with the North – is a retreat, an escape. The
epithet Dickens chose to describe his ending in two letters
he wrote at the time surely underlines that: 'I have just
finished my book (very prettily indeed, I hope)'; and 'I like
the conclusion very much and think it *very pretty indeed.*'
But the Chancery world that he had painted and anat-
omized so convincingly continues just as bleakly.
Tulkinghorn and Krook and Jo and Gridley may be dead,

and the suit of Jarndyce and Jarndyce have melted away with its estate; but the Smallweeds go on, as does Tom-All-Alone's; there will be more interminable Chancery suits, more Gridleys and Miss Flites driven mad by them; and more Jos darkened by ignorance and killed by disease. In comparison with the interconnected horrors of that world and Dickens's genius in bringing them to life, the pastoral ending of *Bleak House* seems unreal and ineffectual: a wish-fulfilment, however understandable.

Chapter 3

Critical reception

With his vast reading public Dickens felt on terms of peculiar intimacy. For no novelist was periodical publication, despite all its difficulties, so congenial. As an amateur actor for much of his writing-life, and a highly successful public reader during the last part of it, he had the keenest awareness of an audience. It is tempting to say that he saw his monthly – and, for some novels, weekly – readers in much the same light. But it is as friends and companions that he addresses them in many of his Prefaces. In the Preface to the Cheap Edition of *The Old Curiosity Shop* he writes of 'the many friends it won me, and the many hearts it turned to me when they were full of private sorrow'; in the original Preface to *Dombey and Son*, after saying farewell to his readers, he acknowledges 'the unbounded warmth and earnestness of their sympathy in every stage of the journey we have just concluded'; in the Preface to *Little Dorrit* he is 'deeply sensible of the affection and confidence that have grown up between us . . . May we meet again!'

This strong relationship with his public had two important effects. Acceptance of the chief tenets of public taste was essential to his continued popularity; and the public, in its turn, had to be convinced of the importance and responsibility of the art he practised, of what he and Forster called 'the dignity of literature'. Delicacy in all sexual references was especially demanded by public taste. Both *Dombey and Son* and *David Copperfield* had offered temptations to defy the conventions; and in both he had resisted them. He had intended to make Edith

Dombey Carker's mistress, but accepted his friend Lord Jeffrey's advice not to do so. In *Copperfield* we are given virtually no details of Steerforth's seduction of Little Emily; and the picture of the prostitute, Martha, is entirely a stereotyped one. By setting the love-affair between Lady Dedlock and Captain Hawdon safely in the past, there could be no danger of any illicit sexual scenes in *Bleak House*. The love-affair between Richard and Ada is highly idealized; that between Woodcourt and Esther, when we are allowed to see it, even more so. John Jarndyce's feelings for Esther appear to be entirely sexless.

Throughout the planning and first part of writing *Bleak House*, Dickens was especially conscious of the status and importance of the professional writer. In 1851 he and his friend, the novelist and politician Sir Edward Bulwer Lytton, founded the Guild of Literature and Art, an insurance society for writers and artists, to help their less fortunate brethren. The amateur theatricals Dickens directed in 1851 and 1852 provided it with most of its endowment. And the language he used in his letters about it shows the strong power 'the dignity of literature' exerted on his imagination. 'We hold in our hands the peace and honour of men of letters for centuries to come', he wrote to Bulwer Lytton; and to Angela Burdett Coutts he reported Lytton as saying to him after one of their theatrical performances: 'This is a great power that has grown up about you, out of a winter-night's amusement, and do let us try to use it for the lasting service of our order.' *Bleak House* is dedicated to 'My Companions in the Guild of Literature and Art'.

K. J. Fielding (in *The Dickensian*, January 1968) was surely right in claiming that allegiance to 'our order', pride in the status of the writer, played its part in the modelling of Skimpole on Leigh Hunt. Hunt was not, in

Dickens's eyes, serious enough about the *professionalism* of literature. It was his Bohemian indulgence, his readiness to be patronized by anyone who would pay for the privilege, that underlay the portrait of him as Skimpole.

Thackeray too was insufficiently serious about the writer's status, for Dickens: it was as much the true cause of their quarrels as jealousy. And it was to Thackeray – in response to a letter that had clearly praised *Dombey and Son* – that in January 1848 Dickens wrote, setting out his aspirations for the writer most strongly:

I *do* sometimes please myself with thinking that my success has opened the way for good writers . . . I am always possessed with the hope of leaving the position of literary men in England something better and more independent than I found it.

Dickens wrote a generous tribute to Thackeray in the *Cornhill Magazine* after his death; but he could not leave their differences over the status of literature alone:

I thought that he too much feigned a want of earnestness, and that he made a pretence of undervaluing his art, which was not good for the art he held in trust.

There can be no question of the 'earnestness' or social purposefulness of *Bleak House*. Dickens was proud to claim it – of all his writing – in a letter to the daughter of Lord Denman, defending Mrs Jellyby from his strictures, written in December 1852:

Pray do not, therefore, be induced to suppose that I ever write merely to amuse, or without an object . . . I may try to insinuate it into people's hearts sometimes, in preference to knocking them down and breaking their heads with it . . . but I always have it. Without it, my pursuit – and the steadiness, patience, seclusion, regularity, hard work, and self-concentration it demands – would be utterly worthless to me. I should die at the oar, and could die a more contemptible death in no man's eyes than in my own.

This sense of purpose had been an integral part of his popularity, especially with working-class readers, since his earliest writing. G. M. Young, in *Early Victorian England* (1934), quotes a remark by a Nonconformist preacher of the 1840s that has become famous:

There have been at work among us three great social agencies: the London City Mission; the novels of Mr Dickens; the cholera.

The reviewer in the *Westminster Review* of 1843 who praised Dickens's 'latest desire to . . . raise the trampled upon, soften intolerance, diffuse knowledge, promote happiness', was typical of many in the period. But *Bleak House* became something of a watershed. For many, its far darker social criticism and more scathing satire were a perversion of his true powers as a novelist, of his gifts for comedy and pathos. For others – and they have become increasingly the majority – *Bleak House* is the first of his greatest novels. A genuine motive for the change in some critics' attitude was aesthetic: the belief that a novel should move and entertain, not preach. But it is obvious that in many cases this disguised political or social resentment; and the area of resentment became increasingly wider. In *Bleak House* the satire on Sir Leicester Dedlock and on Coodle and Doodle as political leaders angered the Conservatives; the satire on Mrs Jellyby and the mission to Africa angered the Liberals. J. S. Mill, a strong feminist, was infuriated by the portrait of Mrs Jellyby:

That creature Dickens, whose last story, *Bleak House*, I found accidentally at the London Library the other day and took home and read – much the worst of his things, and the only one of them I altogether dislike – has the vulgar impudence in this thing to ridicule rights of women. It is done in the very vulgarest way – just the style in which vulgar men used to ridicule 'learned ladies' as neglecting their children and household etc.

It was not in fact until *Little Dorrit* that both the 'aesthetic' and the 'political' critics raised their voices together; but they both included *Bleak House* within their strictures. 'Remonstrance with Dickens', by E. B. Hamley (*Blackwood's Magazine*, April 1857), takes the view that, from *Bleak House* onwards, Dickens has betrayed his true early genius:

we can't wait for the end of the wilderness of *Little Dorrit* before recording our earnest protest and deep lament; for in that wilderness we sit down and weep when we remember thee, O *Pickwick*!

The 'wilderness' extended back to *Bleak House* too: spoiled, for Hamley, like *Little Dorrit*, by Dickens's listening to the 'booby' who persuades him to go 'to the heart of our deepest social problems' and 'another luminary' who tells him 'it is the duty of a great and popular writer to be a great moral teacher'. James Fitzjames Stephen, distinguished lawyer and son of the civil servant, Sir James Stephen, is much more hostile and explicitly political in 'Mr Dickens as a Politician' (*Saturday Review*, January 1857). He is, of course, *parti pris*. Both Jarndyce and Jarndyce and the Circumlocution Office of *Little Dorrit* had deeply offended him; and he treats Dickens as an anarchist or dangerous radical rather than as a novelist:

And yet this man, who knows absolutely nothing of law or politics – who was so ignorant of the one subject that he grumbled at the length of an administration suit (which is like grumbling at the slowness of the lapse of time), and so ignorant of the other that he represented Parliament as a debating club – has elaborated a kind of theory of politics.

Among the critics at the time, there were the usual arguments about plot-construction, exaggeration of characters and incidents, success or lack of success of humour and pathos. Several critics proclaimed the portrait of Jo as the finest writing in the novel. (Many years later Edward Ramsay, Dean of Edinburgh, wrote to Forster: 'To my mind, nothing in the field of fiction is to be found in English literature surpassing the death of Jo!'). But one critic stands out as anticipating much twentieth-century praise of *Bleak House* as a whole and that, appropriately, is Dickens's most intimate friend, John Forster. His unsigned review in the *Examiner* (October 1853) points towards much modern poetic and symbolist criticism of Dickens:

Novels as Mr Dickens writes them rise to the dignity of poems.

Whenever the occasion arises, or the art of the story-teller requires, the thick atmosphere of law that rises out of Jarndyce *v.* Jarndyce is made to cling like a fog about the people in the story. It may be more or less, but there it is. Either as a thick cloud or a light mist, it is to be seen everywhere.

Whatever critics wrote of Dickens's 'decline', it had no visible effect on his sales. *Bleak House* sold over 35,000 copies a Part, 10,000 more than *David Copperfield*; *Edwin Drood* reached 50,000. With the popularity of *Bleak House* Dickens himself was highly satisfied: 'It is a most enormous success', he wrote to a friend in May 1852; 'all the prestige of Copperfield (which was very great) falling upon it, and raising its circulation above all my other books'.

Krook's 'Spontaneous Combustion' played a bizarre rôle in raising the question of Dickens's responsibility as an artist. G. H. Lewes, the consort of George Eliot, distinguished both as scientist and literary critic – and a friend of Dickens – attacked it at once as impossible, and Dickens himself as irresponsibly sensationalist in deluding his readers into believing it could happen. Dickens sought 'authorities' from an eminent medical friend; then defended it, first, in letters to the journal Lewes edited, the *Leader*; then in the next chapter of the novel; and finally in the Preface to the one volume edition, written on its completion. The defence is now accepted as absurd; Lewes was right in his knowledge that spontaneous combustion was scientifically impossible. But the incident illuminates Dickens's determination, as a novelist, to have things both ways. In the argument of the time over realism (or naturalism) and romance, Dickens was several times called an intermediary; seen as occupying a position between the two. But he clearly wanted to be, and to be seen to be, a master of both: to be a realist, vital for writing 'tracts for the times'; *and* to be a romantic, with all the imaginative life and fantasy the romantic tradition fostered. 'In *Bleak House*', he ended his Preface, 'I have purposely dwelt upon the romantic side of familiar things.' Krook's 'Spontaneous Combustion' had to be accepted as fact as well as symbol; just as, in his Preface, he gave the facts of a notorious Chancery case, still undecided (found for him by his assistant editor on *Household Words*), so that Jarndyce and Jarndyce could be seen to be 'true', as well as a monstrous symbol of all the strangling power that Chancery stands for in the novel. Four years after finishing *Bleak House*, in a letter about 'The Tour of Two Idle Apprentices' he had just written with Wilkie Collins, Dickens described some of the descriptions of the tour as 'remarkable for their fanciful fidelity'. The phrase neatly incapsulates his ambition to be master of both factual truth and imaginative life.

Most of those who criticized Dickens's later novels were affronted by what they saw as his lack of naturalism. But it was G. H. Lewes who, in 'Dickens in Relation to Criticism', an essay published in the *Fortnightly Review* in 1872, two years after Dickens's death, developed the kind of naturalist criticism he had launched in the 'spontaneous combustion' controversy into a highly sceptical enquiry into Dickens as a serious novelist at all. His 'glorious energy of imagination' he allowed him; but its creations – above all, his characters – were unreal, falsely distorted: he 'was a seer of visions'; he heard voices; his vividness of imagination approached 'closely to hallucination'. With his immense powers, he totally deluded his readers.

Dickens's vast public was content to be deluded. And again and again Dickens defended the Fancy or Imagination that could achieve this end. We have few direct comments from him on the importance of the novel as literature. But in one, made to Forster, he shows that he knew exactly where, on this central issue, he stood:

in these times, when the tendency is to be frightfully literal and catalogue-like – to make the thing, in short, a sort of sum in reduction that any miserable creature can do in that way – I have an idea (really founded on the love of what I profess), that the very holding of popular literature through a kind of popular dark age, may depend on such fanciful treatment.

Chapter 4

Context in European literature

That last statement of belief goes a long way to establishing Dickens's place as a novelist. He believed intensely in the practicalities of individual and social experience, in what he would have called 'the real' (as Forster stresses throughout his *Life*); and to that extent he was a realist. But he believed, just as intensely, in the novelist's imagination, in his power to shape the reality he observed into his own vision. The label of 'romantic realist' that Donald Fanger adopts in his comparative study, *Dostoevsky and Romantic Realism* (1965), is as justified for Dickens as it is for the other great nineteenth-century novelists he treats: Balzac, Gogol and Dostoevsky himself. For all of them, in varying degrees, romantic 'Nature' has been jettisoned; in its place is the modern city, Paris, London, St Petersburg, with all its mysteries, secrets, mixture of glitter and squalor. Their visions of it are, of course, as different as the three cities themselves; but each makes the city he knows so intimately into what can only be called a myth; and it is the power of this myth, the blend of omniscient detailed knowledge with a powerful imaginative view – generally a mixture of attraction and repulsion – that creates the affinities between them.

With Balzac (1799–1850) and Gogol (1809–52), it is easier to show affinity than direct influence either way. Dickens saw a dramatized version of Balzac's *Old Goriot* in Genoa in 1844 and his comment suggests that he already knew the novel – perhaps well: 'The domestic Lear I thought at first was going to be very clever. But he

94

was too pitiful – perhaps the Italian reality would be.' He must have known other novels of *Là Comédie Humaine*, published between 1830 and 1848; but, although Balzac's *Droll Stories* was in his library at his death and he mentions Balzac once more in a letter, he makes no further comments on him. Gogol's *Dead Souls* was published in 1842 and several Russian critics assumed that Dickens – and especially *The Pickwick Papers* – had been an influence on him. Much later, in 1867, Dickens showed, in a letter to his friend Bulwer Lytton, that he had read at any rate one of Gogol's stories in a French translation. But, as with Balzac, there are no further comments.

With Dostoevsky (1821–81), nine years younger than Dickens, it is different. We know from his diaries, letters and articles that he read and highly admired Dickens. Replying to a friend who had asked him what books he should give his daughter to read, he wrote (in 1880): 'All Dickens's books, absolutely without exception.' That, as Angus Wilson argued in his Dickens Memorial Lecture, 'Dickens and Dostoevsky' (1970), strongly implies that he had read all his novels himself. But it was the early Dickens, up to and including *David Copperfield*, that Dostoevsky knew particularly well (in translation); there are, sadly, no surviving comments on *Bleak House* or on any of the later novels. Several critics have discussed in detail Dostoevsky's debt, in Raskolnikov's murder of the pawnbroker in *Crime and Punishment* (1866), to Jonas Chuzzlewit's murder of Montagu Tigg in *Martin Chuzzlewit*, and particularly in the treatment of Raskolnikov's guilt; likewise, what Dostoevsky owed to Dickens's good and humble characters – especially Mr Pickwick and the Micawbers – in *The Idiot* (1868–9). Again, there are obvious parallels between Steerforth of *David Copperfield* and Stavrogin of *The Devils*.

But the affinity between Dickens and Dostoevsky is much more than a similarity between individuals and incidents. From *Crime and Punishment* on we feel, as Angus Wilson puts it, 'the world of Dickens and the world of Dostoevsky to be the same world'. They share the same sense of the great city, London or St Petersburg, as a living presence; and each marvellously communicates the intense loneliness of the individual – Raskolnikov or Arthur Clennam of *Little Dorrit* – as he walks endlessly through its streets. They share the same sense of absolute evil, and something – although Dostoevsky has the confidence to be much more explicit about it – of the same sense of absolute good. Above all, they each use comedy – often grotesque comedy – seriously; they share the conviction that much of life is, ultimately, tragi-comic. The major ironies of *Bleak House* – Richard's obsession with a system that is destroying him, the revelation that Esther is Lady Dedlock's daughter, Sir Leicester's waiting for a wife who will never return – all these different facets of a tragi-comic universe would have appealed strongly to Dostoevsky.

Much has been made of the similarity between Balzac and Dickens. They were obsessed, respectively, with Paris and London ('Paris is a living thing', said Balzac), and, above all, with the hidden, mysterious life of a great modern city. They are unsurpassed as devourers of fact. Henry James was unjust to them both, but he catches their remarkable imaginative energy: 'they most of all resemble each other in the fact that they treated their extraordinary imaginative force as a matter of business; that they worked it as a gold-mine, violently and brutally; overworked and ravaged it' (*French Poets and Novelists*).

They are unsurpassed too in their use of atmosphere, whether it be the mysteries of the city or contrasts of light and dark or the appearance of certain houses and rooms or the omens provided by the weather. They are equally obsessed with corruption, and particularly the corruption of the unscrupulous hunt for money. They are both drawn to the same forms of writing, particularly in their handling of crises; and, for many shared effects, they each use great theatrical set-scenes, deliberately melodramatic, often sensational: Krook's death, the discovery of the dead Lady Dedlock; Vautrin's arrest, Goriot's prolonged death-bed, in *Old Goriot*. They were both inevitably accused by their critics of exaggeration. Yet a closer comparison between *Bleak House* and *Old Goriot* (1834), one of the finest of the novels of *Là Comédie Humaine*, will show how individual the genius of each novelist ultimately is. Before such a comparison, the point must be made that, although only a quarter of the length of *Bleak House*, *Old Goriot* is as densely packed as anything Balzac wrote.

Both novels owe something to what German criticism has called the *Bildungsroman* tradition: the novelist's portrait of the unfolding self. Goriot is indeed the tragic hero of *Old Goriot*, and the final scenes focus on his tragedy; but the whole novel is seen through the eyes and mind of Rastignac, the poor young law-student (as Balzac himself had been); and it is his ambitions and moral choices that ultimately determine the plot. And here, at once, the contrast with *Bleak House* is striking. Esther Summerson, whose 'progress' we watch from early childhood to marriage, is unerringly aware of the dense life around her and increasingly involved in its tragic complexity herself; but she remains a voice, however sensitive, a point of consciousness; she is virtually will-less, totally free of ambition. Her final happiness with Woodcourt is quite literally Jarndyce's gift to her. Eugène Rastignac, as a study in selfhood, is the opposite. He grows up in the three months of the novel; and he does so through a sequence of wilful ambitions, conscious desires for love, social acceptance and money. All are relentlessly and often comically observed by Balzac: his falling in love first with one married sister, Anastasie, then with the other, Delphine; his vanities and social gaffes; his exploitation of his mother's and sisters' generosity; his successful penetration, through using his remote cousinhood with Mme de Beauséant, of the Faubourg Saint-Germain; his unfeelingness towards his fellow-boarder, Victorine, who falls in love with him. Throughout, we watch the struggles between his ideals and his temptations, his integrity and the corrupt glitter of Paris. Above all, we watch his attempted moral seduction by the ex-convict Collin, *alias* Vautrin. *Bleak House* has its figures of varying evil and menace: Krook, Grandfather Smallweed, Tulkinghorn, Vholes, all representative of some aspect of the enveloping power of Chancery. But Vautrin is quite different. He is gaily cynical, Mephistotelean, utterly corrupt. In his campaign for Rastignac's soul, he cheerfully arranges for a murder to be committed. At the same time, he is by far the most attractive of Madame Vauquer's boarders; we are on his side in the great scene of his arrest; and, like the other boarders, share his scorn of Mlle Michonneau, his sneaking betrayer. He is an intellectual, a 'ferocious logician', the pupil, he boasts, of Rousseau; 'a man less lily-livered than the rest, who dares to raise his voice against the colossal fraud of the Social Contract': 'In short, I stand alone against organized authority with its mass of law-courts and police and revenues to back it up, and I beat it hollow.'

Dickens has no self-conscious social rebel of this kind. In a sense, he does not need one: from *Bleak House* on, his social institutions – the Court of Chancery, the Circumlocution Office, the stock exchange empire of Merdle – proclaim their own rottenness, even if only Merdle destroys himself.

For both Balzac and Dickens, the city itself breeds its own corruption; but the emphasis is very different. *Bleak House* gives us its grimly comic satire of fashionable society: of the 'Dandies' staying at Chesney Wold, of Lady Dedlock's boredom, Sir Leicester's terror that 'the floodgates will open', Volumnia Dedlock and her 'hideous General' in Bath, the supercilious 'Mercury' yawning in the great empty house in London. But it is only a small part of the novel. Parisian high society dominates *Old Goriot*. Balzac is both fascinated and repelled by the details he paints so brilliantly: the balls, the theatre, the sexual intrigues, and, above all, the squalid greediness and jealousies and vanities that underlie it. 'No Juvenal could adequately paint its gilded and bejewelled horror', says Rastignac; and, more shortly, says the Duchess de Langeais, 'Paris is a slough.'

But the *physical* slough of a great city and its environs that so haunts Dickens in *Bleak House* – Tom-All-Alone's, the brickmakers' hovels, the paupers' graveyard – is hardly to be seen in *Old Goriot*. Even if it was there (and Dickens regarded Paris as giving a lesson to London in sanitation), it was not, for Balzac, the real corruption. That, as increasingly for Dickens, was money: the hunt to get it; the wretchedness without it; the power it gives to its possessors. 'Money is life itself, it's the mainspring of everything', cries Goriot. Obsession with money lies at the heart of *Bleak House* too: it unites the lawyers of every status, the money-lender Grandfather Smallweed, the scavenger Krook, even the aesthete Skimpole – with all his claims not to understand it. We are given an insight into its power in Smallweed's ruthless treatment of Trooper George's debt; and into the corruption it breeds in Smallweed's attempted blackmail of Sir Leicester. But, while it pervades the whole novel, both as fact and symbol – as it does in all Dickens's later novels – we are given only a few actual details of financial transactions. Balzac is obsessed with financial details. We know exactly how much money both Rastignac and Goriot have at every stage of the novel. We know how much rent each of Madame Vauquer's boarders pays her; and even what she pays for their dessert. We are given the details of the Baron de Nuncingen's swindles and the mounting debts that Goriot pays for both his daughters. At the most dramatic financial moment in the novel, Vautrin tells Rastignac how much he will receive for consenting to his plot: a million francs from the promised heiress – less 200,000 francs for himself as the price of the murder which will secure her.

Both Balzac and Dickens are masters of interweaving character and ambience, and of the peculiar animism that gives physical appurtenances – houses, rooms, pictures, clothes – as full (or as distorted) a life as their owners. Madame Vauquer is an emanation of her boarding-house, or vice versa; just as Krook is an emanation of his murky, chaotic shop; and that again is an emanation of Chancery. But, compared with the range of *Bleak House*, *Old Goriot* is deliberately restricted in its ambience, almost claustrophobic: virtually the whole action is played out in the boarding-house rooms or in the great houses Rastignac visits. This points to *Bleak House*'s much greater range, social as well as physical. Balzac needs few grades of society to make his tragic or cynical points, outside Madame Vauquer's shabby-genteel boarders, the fashionable world of Paris, his two students – and Vautrin. For the anatomy that *Bleak House* carries out, Dickens gives us almost every class, from the highest to the lowest, of mid-nineteenth-century England.

This lesser social range has, as one would expect, emotional repercussions too. Benevolently comic characters, like the Bagnets – or even mildly satirized ones, like the Bayham Badgers – have little interest for the Balzac of

Old Goriot. His comedy is throughout sharper, more sophisticated, more selfconsciously moral. But in his depiction of the good (and Balzac acknowledged its difficulties), Balzac's stance is firmer than Dickens's. Rastignac's portrait is shot through with irony, though an irony compatible with his genuine love of his family in the country, with his finally resisting Vautrin, and with his being the only character to recognize Goriot's true nobility. Irony is the quality we most miss in the portrait of Esther Summerson. Goriot himself may have at times the kind of sentimentality we associate with Esther: in his memories of his daughters' childhood, or in his child-like joy when Delphine welcomes him to spend the evening with Rastignac and herself (in the rooms he has himself paid to furnish). But his obsession with his daughters – his willingness to strip himself of everything for their sakes – gives his suffering, when it comes, a stature quite beyond sentimentality. 'I who would sell the Father, Son and Holy Ghost to save either of them a tear!', he cries out; and as the novel documents, with pity and terrible irony, what he does sell and how diabolically ungrateful both daughters are, we recognize Balzac's true achievement: the transformation of this clumsy, plebeian retired vermicelli-maker into the situation of Shakespeare's Lear.

Dickens achieves a comparable tragic effect in his picture of the stricken Sir Leicester Dedlock awaiting a wife, fully forgiven her 'sins', who will never return. This, like Balzac's scene of Goriot's death-bed, in which he alternately implores and curses his absent daughters, is one of Dickens's finest achievements. They show that, with all their great differences, the two novelists share a deep belief in human dignity: above all, a dignity in suffering in circumstances that, in the hands of lesser writers, would conspire to blur or destroy it.

One novelist, whose debt to Dickens is apparent and accepted is Wilkie Collins, the master of the English 'sensation novel' during the last half of the nineteenth century. They were close friends from 1853 onwards; and Collins regarded Dickens as the greatest writer of his day. Dickens certainly learnt something himself from Collins's flair for plotting and he admired him from the start: of Collins's second novel, *Hide and Seek* (incidentally, dedicated to him) he wrote: 'I think it far and away the cleverest novel I have ever seen written by a new hand . . . in some respects masterly.' But there can be no doubt of the influence of *Bleak House*, as a complexly plotted 'detective novel', on Collins's two major novels, *The Woman in White* (1860) and *The Moonstone* (1868). Inspector Bucket anticipates *The Moonstone*'s detective, Sergeant Cuff, by sixteen years; although both owe something to Balzac's Vautrin: not the diabolic, anti-social cynic of *Old Goriot*, but the police agent – still sinister – that he is transformed into in later novels. Vautrin himself owes much to the *Mémoires* (1829) of Eugène François Vidocq, a criminal who in fact became chief of the Paris Sûreté. Thus the detective-novel, one of the most popular English Victorian genres, has a mixed and distinguished Anglo-French ancestry. Balzac and Dickens, above all, showed the serious purposes to which such apparent 'sensation'-writing could be put.

A quite different novel *Bleak House* has been compared with is *The Trial*, by Franz Kafka, first published posthumously in Berlin in 1925. There are several temptations to make the comparison. Kafka mentions both reading Dickens and reading about him (probably Forster's *Life*) in his diaries. He has a long note about *David Copperfield*, in which he describes the first chapter of his unfinished novel *America* as 'a sheer imitation of Dickens . . . and the novel as planned even more so'. It is 'above all the method' of *Copperfield*, he says, that has influenced him. 'It was my intention, as I now perceive, to write a Dickens novel.' Dickens's influence on *America* is by now accepted; and several critics have claimed the closeness of Kafka's *The Castle* to the Circumlocution Office in *Little Dorrit*. *The Trial* seems to have just as close affinities with *Bleak House*. Both Kafka and Dickens had had early experience of the Law: Kafka had been trained as a lawyer; Dickens had been a clerk in a solicitor's office and had reported cases in Doctors' Commons. The Law, as a despotic mystery, dominates both novels; its acts and their effects seem quite arbitrary. Its top-hatted agents execute Joseph K. in a deserted quarry at the end of *The Trial*: 'Like a dog!', as he says; in *Bleak House*, the shock of the absorption of the estate of Jarndyce and Jarndyce in legal costs is the final cause of Richard Carstone's death. Although acknowledging that there is no evidence that Kafka had in fact read *Bleak House*, Mark Spilka devotes the longest section of his study, *Dickens and Kafka* (1969), to a comparison of the two novels.

But it seems to me that there is a world of difference between them. In *Bleak House*, the Law is clearly both a system and a symbol. As a system, it has its well-defined context in the historical Court of Chancery, however exaggerated its fictional representation might be (and Dickens did his best to defend it against such a charge); for its first readers, at any rate, it was anchored in fact. As a symbol, the Law stands for the muddle and greed that, for Dickens, characterized almost all English institutions of the 1850s. The Court of *The Trial*, and the Law it administers, are even more obviously symbols, both more absurd and more frightening than those of *Bleak House*. If the Court's arbitrariness – the total injustice of the Whippers and the executioners – has only too clear political overtones, it plainly has *some* religious meaning also – though the religion it evokes is one characterized solely by mystery, tyranny and injustice. Joseph K., as the novel's opening sentence states categorically, has done nothing wrong to justify his arrest. If he is guilty – as everyone with any contact with the Court assumes he is – then he may be guilty only, as some critics believe, of original sin; it is in any case a sufficient 'guilt', as one of his arresters says, to attract the Law to him. Because of his state, his being, he will irrevocably be punished – and he will do little to prevent it. Much of the novel, in fact, focuses on his increasing helplessness. In the penultimate chapter, 'In the Cathedral', Joseph K. is now alone with a priest, and the priest tells him the story of the man who begs admittance to the Law from the door-keeper who stands before it. Two things the priest says suggest a possible religious analogy. The man, as he nears death, perceives 'a radiance that streams inextinguishably from the door of the Law'; and, just before he dies, the door-keeper answers his question as to why he is alone: 'No one but you could gain admittance through this door, since this door was intended only for you.' But, adds the door-keeper: 'I am now going to shut it.' It is difficult to see any religious sanction in this. It appears totally arbitrary.

Spilka, to me, gives overmuch weight to the religious context of *The Trial*; and, to draw Dickens closer to Kafka, he claims that, in *Bleak House*, 'Dickens gives a pseudo-religious cast to the law which magnifies its horrors.' The horrors of Chancery – Miss Flite's madness, Gridley's obsession and death, Richard's ruin and death also – are bleak enough; but it is a *secular* bleakness, born of the coils of human nature at its worst. Kenge and Carboy's office may *look* 'like an entrance to a church', as Spilka says; but this only emphasizes the grotesque parody of ritual that Chancery spends year after year enacting. Above all, Jarndyce and Jarndyce is a civil action, not a criminal one; the Lord Chancellor sits realistically and visibly in his Court – Joseph K. never even sees the Judge who sentences him. And the lawyers employed by Richard and by Joseph K. underline the distinction between the two Laws even more strikingly. Fees appear to be of no concern to Advocate Huld of *The Trial*; while the motives of the sinister Vholes are entirely financial – he preys on Richard like a vampire, and the end is always money.

Another striking difference between the two novels is their treatment of sexual relationships. As has been said already, there is – and could be, for a novelist so dependent on his public – little overtly sexual in *Bleak House*. The plot is based on an illicit love-affair, with its fruits in an illegitimate child; but that is in the past: Lady Dedlock is hardly a sexual figure in the novel itself. Joseph K.'s sexual temptations, frustration and occasional success are central to *The Trial*, woven into its fabric. The first section ends with his passionately kissing Fraülein Bürstner; she, or someone closely resembling her, is the last figure he sees in the streets, when he is led off to execution. There is the washer-woman, shared by her husband (the Court usher) and the student, and an equal temptation to the Examining Magistrate and to Joseph K. himself; it is she who lets him see the 'law-books' left in the Court: in fact, crudely obscene drawings and a pornographic novel. Leniy, Advocate Huld's webb-fingered nurse, seduces Joseph K. on his first visit to the Advocate and they make love on future visits. There is Elsa, the cabaret-dancer prostitute, whom Joseph K. visits once a week. And, most disturbingly, there are the precociously debauched and knowing young girls of thirteen or less, who flock around him when he visits the painter Titorelli: they belong (like the washer-woman), Titorelli tells him, to the Court.

Both Kafka and Dickens, it is true, are masters of the grotesque. They are also masters of a kind of writing that suggests a further unspoken (sometimes unspeakable) reality behind it. We are more familiar with this in *The Trial*. Careful, often dead-pan, description suddenly reveals a new, nightmarish life behind the objects described: the row of bearded old men in the Court; the extraordinary tableau of whipper and victims in the Bank's lumber-room that is unchanged when Joseph K. opens the door the next day; the entrance to the painter's tenement-house, with its 'disgusting yellow fluid', its escaping rats and bawling infant, that suddenly becomes an opening to Hell. *Bleak House* has its own momentary vision of Hell too, as the night-dwellers of Tom-All-Alone's surround Inspector Bucket and Snagsby. But the technique Dickens mostly relies on, to suggest the unspoken reality behind, is nearer melodrama. Lady Dedlock, as the guilt floods in on her of having *wanted* to murder Tulkinghorn; Esther, as she imagines her mother's body being lifted out of the Thames: both, in their terrified self-communings, are subjects of melodrama. But the reality behind is more deeply buried: it is a state of mind, the ultimate loneliness of the human being. In such scenes Dickens and Kafka come closest. But there are still important distinctions to be made.

Both Dickens's and Kafka's most haunting – and haunted – characters transcend realism in their embodiment of obsessions. But Dickens's narrative has two levels of consciousness (in *Bleak House*, formally so): the character's own and the omniscient narrator's; Kafka's has only one, that of the bewildered 'hero'. Hence (an important point made by Roy Pascal in a *Listener* talk in 1956) Dickens can *free* his hero or heroine, allow David Copperfield and Esther and, later, Arthur Clennam and Pip, to advance from bewilderment to understanding, to achieve clarity. Kafka's characters remain obsessed and bewildered; they are not allowed to develop; and we share their paranoia to the end. And, finally, *The Trial* is focused entirely on Joseph K.'s consciousness; for all his twentieth-century representativeness, Kafka's own anguish is never far away. The individual consciousness – Lady Dedlock's, Esther's, Richard's – is an integral part of *Bleak House*; but it is never Dickens's total interest. In its anatomy of a whole society, the size of its canvas and its architectonic power, *Bleak House* is a social novel in ways that *The Trial*, in the intensity of its central vision, is not – and perhaps does not need to be.

Guide to further reading

(Place of publication is London, unless otherwise stated.)

The most accessible modern editions of Dickens are the New Oxford Illustrated Dickens (1947–58), with the original illustrations (the text of *Bleak House* used here); and the Penguin (1966–). The annotated Norton Critical Edition of *Bleak House*, ed. George Ford and Sylvère Monod, New York, 1977, contains useful background material and a selection of criticism.

The standard biography of Dickens is his *Life* by his closest friend, John Forster, 3 vols., 1872–4. The edition used here is that edited by J. W. T. Ley, in one volume, 1928. The two most recent biograhies are by Edgar Johnson, *Charles Dickens: His Tragedy and Triumph*, 2 vols., New York, 1952 (revised edition, without the critical chapters, one volume, 1977); and by Norman and Jeanne MacKenzie, *Dickens: A Life*, Oxford, 1979. They both incorporate much more material.than Forster, beginning his *Life* only two years after Dickens's death, was able to use. Letters of Dickens quoted are from the Nonesuch Edition of Dickens' Works (*Letters*, 3 vols., 1938); and, up to 1849, from the Pilgrim Edition of his *Letters*, ed. M. House, G. Storey and K. Tillotson, vols. 1–5, 1965–81.

General studies of Dickens (in chronological order)

Edmund Wilson, 'Dickens: the Two Scrooges' in his *The Wound and the Bow*, Cambridge (Mass.) 1941. Still one of the most influential critical essays on Dickens of the last fifty years.

Humphry House, *The Dickens World*, 1941 (reprinted 1960). Indispensable for the historical background.

George Ford, *Dickens and his Readers*, Princeton, 1955. The most useful study of the general critical reception of the novels.

John Butt and Kathleen Tillotson, *Dickens at Work*, 1957 (reprinted 1963 and 1968). Includes 'The topicality of *Bleak House*' drawn on extensively in ch. 1.

K. J. Fielding, *Charles Dickens*, 1958 (2nd edn, 1965). An excellent critical introduction to the novels.

The Dickens Critics, ed. George Ford and Lauriat Lane, Jnr, Cornell, 1961 contains the best-known essays on Dickens, of which George Orwell, 'Charles Dickens', Dorothy Van Ghent, 'The Dickens world', and Angus Wilson, 'Charles Dickens: a haunting', all relate to some aspect of *Bleak House*.

Philip Collins, *Dickens and Crime*, 1962. Includes a useful discussion of Inspector Bucket.

Robert Garis, *The Dickens Theatre*, 1965. The best study of Dickens's theatrical style.

Grahame Smith, *Dickens, Money and Society*, 1968. Of obvious importance to *Bleak House*.

F. R. and Q. D. Leavis, *Dickens the Novelist*, 1970. Q. D. Leavis's essays on *Bleak House* contains one of the first defences of Esther Summerson.

H. P. Sucksmith, *The Narrative Art of Charles Dickens*, 1970. Uses the MSS, memorandum notes and corrected proofs of the novels to show Dickens as a highly conscious narrative artist.

Philip Collins, *Dickens: The Critical Heritage*, 1971. Includes a wide selection of the contemporary reviews of *Bleak House*.

Michael Goldberg, *Carlyle and Dickens*, 1972. Shows the great importance of Carlyle's ideas to Dickens.

Allan Grant, *A Preface to Dickens*, 1984. An excellent introduction in the Longmans Preface Books.

Studies and criticism of Bleak House

Some of the best criticism of *Bleak House* has appeared in collections:
Twentieth-century Interpretations of Bleak House, ed. J. Kong, New Jersey, 1966.
Dickens: Bleak House: A Casebook, ed. A. E. Dyson, 1969.
The Dickensian, 69 (1973): a number devoted to *Bleak House*.

Other recommended studies (in chronological order)

J. Hillis Miller, in *Charles Dickens: The World of his Novels*, 1958.

Morton D. Zabel, '*Bleak House*: the undivided imagination', in *The Dickens Critics* (above).

Grahame Smith, *Bleak House*, Studies in English Literature no. 54, 1974.

Robert Newsom, *Dickens on the Romantic Side of Familiar Things; Bleak House and the Novel Tradition*, 1977.

P. J. M. Scott, '*Bleak House*: the hidden world', in his *Reality and Comic Confidence in Charles Dickens*, 1979.

Comparative studies

Donald Fanger, *Dostoevsky and Romantic Realism*, Harvard, 1965. Discusses Balzac, Dickens, and Gogol, as well as Dostoevsky.

Mark Spilka, *Dickens and Kafka*, Gloucester, Mass., 1969.
Roy Pascal, 'Dickens and Kafka', *The Listener*, 26 Apr. 1956.
Angus Wilson, 'Dickens and Dostoevsky', *Dickens Memorial Lectures*, 1970.